THE MAGIC MOM

What People Are Saying About *The MAGIC Mom*...

"Are you ready to be motivated, challenged, and inspired? Those feelings nearly jump off every page of Alyce Dailey's brilliant new release, *The MAGIC Mom*. I've been privileged to have a front row seat for this journey over the years, having known Alyce since she was a young, single university student. So the dazzling results of her motherhood are not surprising to me at all. Alyce embodies one of the most successful and balanced entrepreneurs I have ever known. Though I myself have been privileged to raise two entrepreneurial sons, I have celebrated her out-of-the-box-insight with her extraordinary daughters. I've even vacationed with them on occasion and witnessed her "magic principles" on a 24/7 basis. So, get a good cup of coffee and a comfortable chair. You are in for a transparent and transformative look at the 'MAGIC' that has shaped the lives of four absolutely mind-blowing young women. Happy life-change!"

DR. JEANNE MAYO

FOUNDER & PRESIDENT OF YOUTH LEADER'S COACH,

THE CADRE,

PLATINUM LEADERSHIP COACHING,

PREVAIL WOMEN'S MASTERMIND,

AUTHOR AND INTERNATIONAL PUBLIC COMMUNICATOR

"In *The MAGIC Mom*, Alyce lays out a new model for mothers to connect with their daughters and change their trajectory. Being a mom is my greatest honor and reading this book reinforced the power we hold. Every mom must read!"

—KARA AYALA, FOUNDER OF REIGN&CO,

FEMALE INVESTOR CLUB

"If anyone is qualified to teach you how to unlock your natural gifts to raise entrepreneurial daughters, it is Alyce Dailey. The real proof is in her extraordinary daughters. Beyond their entrepreneurial accomplishments, it is their character, maturity, and uncommon generosity that I continue to be amazed by. If you are a mom, you owe it to yourself and your girls to learn Alyce's approach to becoming a MAGIC Mom."

—HAL ELROD, #1 BESTSELLING AUTHOR, *THE MIRACLE MORNING, AND THE MIRACLE EQUATION*

"Parenting and entrepreneurship are not for the faint of heart and as Alyce points out, motherhood is one of the most entrepreneurial ventures out there. I'm a big believer that the difference between a good life and a great life is a series of subtle mindset shifts. Alyce so beautifully illustrates the shifts she made in her thinking and that you can too. She went from just surviving to truly thriving in life and as a mom. Through her thoughtfully designed questions at the end of each chapter, she will gently guide you to do the same for yourself and your children. I'm also a big fan of acronyms and now that I know what 'MAGIC' stands for, I'm excited for more of it to show up for me and my family."

—LINDSAY MCCARTHY, CO-AUTHOR OF *THE MIRACLE MORNING FOR PARENTS AND FAMILIES*

"Amazing! We couldn't put the book down! *The MAGIC Mom* is full of authenticity, great wisdom, and practical applications for every season. Even with our daughter being a young woman in college, we found a ton of 'magic' within its pages that we will be sharing with her on her journey."

—IVELISSE PAGE, EXECUTIVE DIRECTOR
& CO-FOUNDER, BELIEVE BIG
—JIMMY PAGE, SPEAKER AND AUTHOR OF THE BESTSELLING
BOOK, *ONE WORD THAT WILL CHANGE YOUR LIFE*

"Alyce Dailey is such an incredible woman and role model. She embodies each of the characteristics that the acronym 'MAGIC' stands for in her groundbreaking book, *The MAGIC Mom*. Her leadership and mentorship are having such a profound impact."

—JUSTIN DONALD, #1 NATIONAL BEST-SELLING
AUTHOR AND FOUNDER OF *THE LIFESTYLE INVESTOR*,
HOST OF *THE LIFESTYLE INVESTOR PODCAST*

"*The MAGIC Mom* is full of authenticity, vulnerability, and practicality. Alyce has 4 gorgeous, intelligent, self-sufficient daughters. I love this niche. It's a much-needed guide for all Moms raising young women."

—WENDY PAPASAN, CHAIRMAN, HER BEST LIFE

"*The MAGIC Mom* is a much needed, powerful book both for mothers and daughters who want to pursue their dreams and do good in the world. Alyce lays out a new model of parenting and framework for mothers to connect with their daughters at a deep heart-centered level and change their trajectory. I loved the focus on cultivating an entrepreneurial spirit, sacred space for courageous growth and teaching that any goal is possible. This is definitely a must-read book for any mom eager to foster emotional health and wellbeing."

—JULIE REISLER, MASTER LIFE COACH, AUTHOR, TEDX SPEAKER, PODCASTER

"If the greatest burden on a child is the unlived life of a parent, as Jung suggests, Alyce's words were written to ensure mothers will live a contrarian life - a life full of pursuing dreams and teaching their daughters to do the same."

—LAURA SANDEFER, CO-FOUNDER, ACTON ACADEMY AND AUTHOR OF *COURAGE TO GROW*

THE MAGIC MOM

5 PRINCIPLES TO UNLOCK YOUR NATURAL GIFTS TO RAISE ENTREPRENEURIAL DAUGHTERS

ALYCE DAILEY

NEW DEGREE PRESS
COPYRIGHT © 2022 ALYCE DAILEY
All rights reserved.

THE MAGIC MOM
5 Principles to Unlock Your Natural Gifts to Raise Entrepreneurial Daughters

ISBN   979-8-88504-522-3 *Paperback*
           979-8-88504-852-1 *Kindle Ebook*
           979-8-88504-528-5 *Ebook*

*For Seth—the MAGIC Dad and my partner
in life, love, and all the things.*

*And to our four amazing girls—Karissa, Lorra, Annika, and
Brielle. You girls are the best gifts that God knew we needed.*

Table of Contents

AUTHOR'S NOTE 21

PART I.   MODEL **33**
CHAPTER 1.   MINDSET 41
CHAPTER 2.   LEAD 53
CHAPTER 3.   GOALS 63

PART II.   AFFIRM **75**
CHAPTER 4.   COMMUNITY 83
CHAPTER 5.   VALUES 93
CHAPTER 6.   GO 103

PART III. GRACE **117**
CHAPTER 7.   TRAUMA 127
CHAPTER 8.   BUSY 141
CHAPTER 9.   EMPATHY 157

PART IV.   INQUIRE **167**
CHAPTER 10. EDUCATION 173
CHAPTER 11. TRADITIONS 189
CHAPTER 12. CHANGE 201

PART V.   COACH **209**
CHAPTER 13. ROLES 215
CHAPTER 14. FAILURE 225
CHAPTER 15. ACT 235

A LETTER TO YOU, MOM	243
A NOTE TO MY FOUR AMAZING GIRLS	245
ACKNOWLEDGMENTS	251
APPENDIX	259
RESOURCES	263
ABOUT THE AUTHOR	267

"Mothers have martyred themselves in their children's names since the beginning of time. We have lived as if she who disappears the most, loves the most. We have been conditioned to prove our love by slowly ceasing to exist.

"...(Our daughters) will believe they have permission to live only as fully as their mothers allowed themselves to live.

"...When we call martyrdom love we teach our children that when love begins, life ends. This is why Jung suggested: There is no greater burden on a child than the unlived life of a parent."

—GLENNON DOYLE, UNTAMED

MAGICal Notes from My Daughters

KARISSA (AGE EIGHTEEN)

As a kid, I had some incredible experiences. I traveled alone starting at twelve years old. I navigated big, new cities alone—without a phone or a map. I spoke on stage in front of hundreds of people. I learned how to set goals and create vision boards. I attended personal growth events and walked across fire. I networked and developed relationships with mentors who pushed me in all areas of life. I wasn't raised like most kids, and the reason is because my mom is not like most moms.

Now being an adult and looking back at my life, I can say I was empowered more than most kids my age. I was raised by parents who trusted me and gave me the space to make decisions and accept responsibility for my own actions. I would not be who I am today had my parents not raised me as intentionally as they did. To pinpoint the one thing that my parents did differently is hard for me, but I know this: I was raised in a pretty special way, filled with lots of MAGIC.

For the mom who just picked up this book, let me be the first to congratulate you on this new adventure and journey you get to take! As a daughter nothing is more inspiring than watching my mom grow and improve herself, and that is exactly what you are modeling for your own child.

My mom is my best friend, my biggest cheerleader, and my most trusted advisor. But the road to get here was not easy. I hope you can learn and feel inspired from the successes and failures from the last eighteen years of our journey together. Above all, my biggest hope is that you feel empowered as a mom and that you, too, become best friends with your daughter—just like my mom and me!

LORRA (AGE SIXTEEN)
We are watching.

We look to you to show us the way. You are our standard of what we should expect for ourselves and what standards to hold. I started to realize that the standards I allowed for myself mimicked what my mom did for herself. She always led by her actions. She did not, for example, tell her daughters to follow their dreams and then enslave herself to a nine-to-five job she did not love. My mom took action herself without telling her daughters what to do, trusting that we would catch on. Trusting that actions speak louder than words.

I've learned from my mom that knowing *how* to think is more important than knowing *what* to think. Instead of giving me a "do" and "don't do" list, she was inquisitive and asked me questions. With this type of guidance, I've been able to build a framework of how to think and feel confident that I can find my way when I face an unprecedented challenge.

I've always looked up to my mom, and because of everything she's done for herself and for our family, I always will. The life she lives reminds me of what I am capable of, and I hope I can do the same for those who matter most to me.

ANNIKA (AGE THIRTEEN)

My love language is quality time, and my mom really gets that about me. We love having special time together doing things most people might find odd, but I love them. We just have fun being together, whether it's going to the grocery store or running an errand.

A favorite memory is when we went to Cancun as a family and my mom and I snuck away to get my favorite dessert together before dinner. My mom has been great about teaching me the value of experiences and money from a young age. Another favorite memory is going to see Tony Robbins with my dad, and I'm thankful my parents invested in the opportunity for me. I'm proud to be the youngest Dailey to have completed it!

Our family is awesome, and I'd say my mom is pretty slay. Sometimes I call her the slay queen boss. She is caring, thoughtful, and adventurous, and I'm glad to have her as my mom.

BRIELLE (AGE TEN)

I love our family and that we go on lots of adventures. It's fun when I try something new and we get to do it together. I missed my mom when she went to climb Mount Kilimanjaro when I was little. I remember crying when she left. But climbing a mountain is super coolio and a big achievement. My mom is adventurous and courageous.

I want to write a book like my mom one day. I love that she works from home and I get to see her a lot. My mom is thoughtful and funny. I love her because she cares so much about others.

Author's Note

As a Girl Mom four times over, I hear some awfully asinine remarks from others on a regular basis.

My husband and I sat down at a bar at an upscale restaurant, and the lady next to us struck up a conversation when she realized we were new to the area. Upon hearing that we have four daughters, the all too familiar lines began pouring out.

"Oh my gosh… I am so sorry!" (This is by *far* the most common.)

"How do you do it?"

"You never got that boy?"

"God bless you!"

"I can't imagine that many women in one house!"

"How many of them are *teenagers*?"

"Just wait until they don't like you anymore!"

"Wow! All of those hormones and cycles at the same time!"

"Your poor husband!"

"Well, that will cost you a fortune!"

We live in a world that still believes having a son is more desirable than having a daughter, even in the West. It has gone on for ages—from the beginning of time—and, as evidenced by these comments, this belief is sadly still very much alive and kicking.

Twenty years ago, or even before, if you had told me I would be the mom of four daughters, I would have laughed mercilessly at you. In my little symmetrical thinking head, I knew that I'd have at least one girl and one boy. Thankfully I didn't have millions of dollars to place a bet, or I would have surely lost it all. As it turns out, being a Girl Mom four times over is the absolute greatest gift I never knew I wanted or needed.

Raising four daughters has been the purest joy of my life. As I've traveled across the country to conferences, masterminds, and retreats, the number one question I've been asked over the years is this: "How have you managed to raise such amazing girls?"

For years, I would just shrug my shoulders and say something trite like, "I'm just really lucky." But, as I've stopped to delve into the real answer, I've realized it isn't luck at all.

So then, what exactly is it?

From my mentors over the years, I've learned that success leaves clues. And, as I've looked back over the past twenty years in my own momhood journey, I see some distinct patterns.

Our girls are eighteen, sixteen, thirteen, and ten years old. They are confident, well-spoken, and leaders in their own different ways. They think for themselves, and we have deep conversations in our home, which could rival those of the best graduate students. They are well-traveled and curious. They possess an entrepreneurial spirit.

Before we get any further, it's important that we take an interlude and define what we mean by "entrepreneur" and understand why instilling the entrepreneurial spirit in our daughters is something to be desired and developed.

An entrepreneur, according to *Merriam-Webster's* online edition, is "a person who organizes and manages any enterprise, especially a business, usually with considerable initiative and risk."

Any enterprise—with *initiative and risk*. The words "initiative and risk" exhilarate some of you and spark fear for others, like me. I was terrified of entrepreneurship yet fully aware something was magical about it, and I believed that lots of freedom and opportunity could be found through its pursuit.

Male entrepreneurs are a dime a dozen. No one bats an eye when a guy says he's going to start a business or get an MBA or take out a massive loan the size of Montana. When a girl wants to start a business, she is often subject to comments a male typically doesn't hear, like:

"Be careful! Starting a business is hard. Most people fail in their first five years. Are you sure you don't just want to get a 'real' job?"

"Don't you want to get married and start a family?"

"Is it really wise to start a business now?"

However, the entrepreneurial spirit is not limited to those who want to start their own business. I believe being a mom is, in fact, the most entrepreneurial venture that exists on the planet. Talk about managing an enterprise and taking risks without a guidebook!

As an entrepreneur who has started businesses and who has coached entrepreneurs for years, one of the most sought-after qualities in those whom entrepreneurs are looking to hire is the entrepreneurial spirit. Entrepreneurs can (and should) exist *within* every organization. These individuals are known as "intrapreneurs," as they are growing and building within an existing structure.

The world holds countless opportunities, and those who possess an entrepreneurial spirit are best positioned to seize the opportunities life throws their way. The entrepreneurial spirit will serve your daughter absolutely anywhere she chooses to go in life.

Raising entrepreneurial-spirited young women in today's increasingly complex world has also been the catalyst for my own personal growth and exploration into my calling and purpose. For example, as I've sought to help them grow, I've found it was necessary to put on my own oxygen mask first.

Looking back over the past twenty years, I can trace my *"momming"* success to something I call MAGIC:

Model
Affirm
Grace
Inquire
Coach

Truly every remarkable, risky initiative I've tackled as a mom has its roots in this acronym. And I've done a lot as a mom. More specifically, my family has done a lot of remarkable things together. We've started multiple businesses together and separately, invested in real estate, stocks, and cryptocurrency, and bought our dream home where we can host retreats. Since our girls were very small, my husband and I have brought them with us as attendees at countless personal and professional development conferences. My daughters have joined us as we walked on fire, broke planks with our hands, created vision boards, and became certified as Master Practitioners in Neurolinguistic Programming. We've moved away from traditional education, transplanted ourselves across the country, expanded our friend circles, and gotten a puppy or two. We recently sent one daughter to Puerto Rico for an apprenticeship opportunity, built a food forest in our yard, took epic road trips in our new RV, and we are working on turning part of home into an Airbnb. I have taken on some challenging adventures of my own, including writing books, changing careers, and climbing Mount Kilimanjaro. Oh, and did I mention having four classical C-sections and raising some epic daughters?

It all started with **MAGIC**.

And this is where you come in, Mom.

Entrepreneurship is about taking on any enterprise—with initiative and risk. That doesn't just mean a business. This could be an educational pursuit, a new career, a new relationship, or starting a family. All of these are entrepreneurial in nature, so why don't we treat them as such? What if we considered that many of the skills needed to run a business are the same ones that are needed to run a household or to boost a career?

Being a mom *is* the most entrepreneurial venture you could ever take on, based on the very definition of entrepreneur. As you read these pages, I encourage you to embrace the identity of the entrepreneur you already are—just by virtue of being a mom. Is anything riskier than bringing a daughter into the world and raising her to be a next-generation leader?

I believe you picked up this book because you believe in giving your daughter better coaching than you had as a young girl—a life better than you had in some way.

I believe you have a deep desire for your daughter to create a life where she can be truly happy and free.

I believe you have untapped potential yourself that is ready to be unleashed.

I believe you might be scared to death, feeling like you're inadequate to do the job set before you.

May I offer you some hope?

You're not inadequate. You're just ill-equipped. And there's a world of difference between the two.

Did you hear me? You're just ill-equipped. And I was too. No one gave you the tools to pursue this entrepreneurial spirit, so how could you give them to your daughter?

Does it mean that your daughter needs to go start the next Google? No. But wouldn't it be awesome to know that she has the skills to do it if she so chooses? And you, my friend, can help develop these in her. How? That's what we're going to talk about.

I wasn't given the tools by my family of origin, but through thousands of dollars and hours spent over the past three decades, I've landed on some pretty timeless and solid knowledge I'd be honored to share so you can take some shortcuts.

Disclaimer: As I found myself being asked some of the same questions over and over again about things we've done to raise girls who have some pretty awesome traits, I'll be the first to admit that my girls are far from perfect (as am I).

Our family doesn't have all of our stuff together. We're a mess. A beautiful mess, but a mess nonetheless. I'm the mom who was so freaking proud of myself that I remembered to schedule our fourth daughter's twenty-four-month doctor's appointment within the correct quarter of the year... only to be told that I had missed her twelve- and eighteen-month appointments. I've done lots of traveling for business and missed school concerts. I've forgotten to pick up a kid a time or two (or more). I've let them eat chicken nuggets and mac 'n' cheese too many times in a row for dinner due to my own exhaustion. We've gotten a lot of things wrong. And, I'm still on the journey of raising them. But I think, overall, we've gotten more right than not. And lots of the tools and tricks we've picked up along the way are worth spreading.

HOW TO USE THIS BOOK
The idea of **MAGIC** is one of self-reflection. It isn't just about something to "do" but rather a reflection into who we are as women and moms.

My mission is to equip moms to become the best version of themselves so they can equip the next generation of women to be healthy and whole. This starts right in our homes. It starts with you and your daughter. I want you to be able to take risks to live a life you love and be able to teach your daughter the skills to do the same. How does building a life you don't need a vacation from sound to you? Pretty good? Then keep reading.

I've been blessed with four amazing young women in our home. Although they are obviously sisters from their mere appearances, they are all as different as the day is long. Yet we've been able to nurture some traits that will serve each of them well as they prepare to leave the nest.

This book is broken up into stand-alone chapters that don't necessarily need to be read in sequence if you're the type of person who likes to skip around. Each chapter ends with some reflection questions that I hope you'll create space to ponder.

Read this book with the intention to actively reflect on it. We've been sold a false bill of goods that "knowledge is power." It isn't. Knowledge is *potential* power. If knowledge was in fact power, librarians and professors would be among the most powerful people in the world.

We've been taught to believe that learning and change comes from just taking information in. The reality, however, is that the learning comes from the reflection on what we've internalized and how we apply it to our own lives. There will be questions to reflect. Allow your brain and heart to move into a place of quiet and listening. Grab a journal and doodle your thoughts and feelings as they come up. No need to judge them, just get them out and let the process of reflection and creativity flow, even if you don't understand it. As Rumi says, "There is a voice that doesn't use words. Listen."

Knowledge becomes power when we add in action. We must act in order to experience power. If you're like me, you'll want the action to be perfect. I'm here to tell you to just act—no matter how imperfect the action. This stuff still works. And the more you experience it working, the more of it you'll want to do and the better you'll become at doing it.

Finally, lasting life change comes in the application of these ideas within a community. And, yes, we have one for you if you're looking to find some new friends on your journey!

If you're newer to personal growth, this process may feel uncomfortable—and that's great! When's the last time you did something new and it wasn't uncomfortable? As one of my daughters says often and has posted in her locker, "A comfort zone is a beautiful place. But nothing ever grows there."

If you've been in the personal growth world for a while, I encourage you to dive deeper. It's all about peeling back the layers. My goal is to help you discover more about how you're wired so you can make an impact that multiple generations to come will feel the positive ripples. Even if you've done some of these exercises before, acknowledge that you aren't the same person today as you were before. I challenge you to see how you've grown since the last time and to reflect even more deeply on your path ahead.

Once you've completed the book, you'll start to see MAGIC show up all over the place in your life. When you hit a challenge or an uncomfortable place, just come back to it:

M (**Model**): How am I modeling who I want my daughter to be as an adult? Who is a model for me in this season?

A (**Affirm**): What affirmation can I speak aloud to allow my subconscious to help me find the answers I need?

G (**Grace**): Who can I extend grace to in this situation and moment?

I (**Inquire**): What new questions could I ask to open up more possibility?

C (**Coach**): How am I showing up as a coach to my daughter right now? Who is coaching me to become the best version of myself?

All of the answers—and questions—that you need to solve your challenge are within you. And just like Dorothy in *The Wizard of Oz*, you already have everything in you to get home. Sometimes a little MAGIC is all we need to help us get there.

Remember our mission? It's to equip you to become the best version of yourself so you can equip the next generation of women to be healthy and whole in order to face the challenges they will encounter. Go ahead and take some risks to live a life you love, and you'll empower your daughter to do the same. You'd be willing to die for her. Wouldn't you? So how about you take some risks to fully live for her—and for you—too?

Get your journal and even a girlfriend to go with you down this road. Journeys like this one are best taken with a friend if you can. And be sure to find me and some new friends as well on social media and at www.TheMAGICMom.com. When you've finished, please share your story of MAGIC with me and with our community. I know you'll inspire others on the journey and find a little inspiration on the way too.

I'm honored to be on this MAGICal journey with you.

xo—
Alyce

PART ONE:

MODEL

"I think the best role models for women are people who are fruitfully and confidently themselves who bring light into the world."

—MERYL STREEP

In every home Seth and I have lived in for the past twenty-two years, even to this day, you can walk into our kitchen and find tucked inside a cabinet a reusable, plastic grocery bag with about ninety-seven million plastic grocery bags inside. I keep them all. Every single bag that has come home from the grocery store makes its way to die in this kitchen cabinet. On occasion, I'll have need for one of these bags and will take great pride in using one although they obviously accumulate much more quickly than they are ever needed. One thing is for certain: They do *not* get wasted by ending up in the trash.

If you go into my mom's kitchen, you'll see the same thing. She has a bag with all the bags in it. Bags that go back to probably 1983, when we moved into that home. Bags from stores that are long out of business.

If I've absorbed this seemingly trivial and insignificant habit from my mom, it is a certainty that I've modeled, consciously and unconsciously, other things that are much more important too.

If it's true that a primary way children learn is by imitating, who and what we imitate matters.

Am I the kind of adult I want my daughter to be?

I ask myself this pivotal underlying question often. It's a haunting question.

My daughters are usually too busy watching what I'm doing to actually ever hear what I'm saying. So if that's true, it means the concept of modeling mindset and actions is vital.

Models are proof that success leaves clues. Models are the legal way to cheat and a loophole to be used. Don't want to reinvent the proverbial wheel? Me neither. I have no interest in doing more work than necessary, and I'm guessing you're in the same boat. Models allow us to stand on the shoulders of the giants that came before us. It gives us a shortcut to the Gumdrop Forest in a game of Candy Land.

Merriam-Webster defines a model in some of the following ways:

- an example for imitation or emulation
- a person or thing that serves as a pattern for an artist *especially*: one who poses for an artist
- serving as or capable of serving as a pattern

Who you want your daughter to be actually begins with who *you* are. Have you ever said to your daughter something like, "Just do what I tell you!" I have. And moments later I'm reliably flooded with some sort of shame and anger because I feel like a hypocrite. I want them to do it one way when I know I haven't exactly modeled the behavior I'm asking from them.

My daughters are more in tune with what I'm doing than they are with the words I say. It's just plain human nature. Actions speak louder than words. According to the world-renowned psychological researcher on nonverbal communication, Dr. Albert Mehrabian at UCLA, only seven percent of the actual words spoken are ever received by the listener. Our actions and being matter. More of what they learn is *caught* rather than taught.

When my girls were little, they loved playing dress-up… out of *my* closet. Dresses, heels, jewelry, makeup—the whole nine yards. They would even talk on pretend cell phones, and I would overhear them negotiating contracts with clients. Every parent has overheard similar types of adorable mimicry, only to be horrified that their children are watching *everything*! They are simply modeling what they are seeing us do, and they want to do the same.

Ever have a friend with a little kid who uses an off-color word? Where do you think they learned it? Immediately the mom will get flustered and say, "I told you not to say that!" But they were too intent on watching their model and emulating her. They were not merely, or even primarily, listening to the words being used. Whatever we do in moderation, we give our daughter permission to do in excess.

Let's start here. What are some words that come to mind when you think about who you want your daughter to be when she's older?

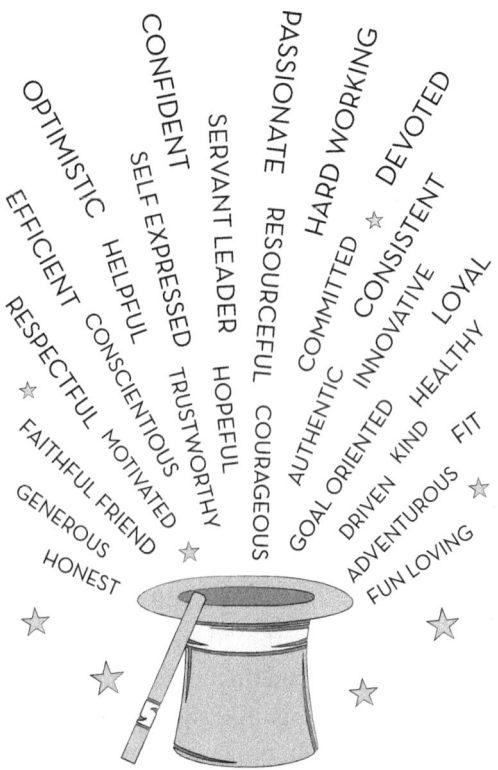

This is just a small sampling of all of the things your daughter could be. Could your daughter be all of those things? Yes! But only if she first knows what these words mean in real life.

She needs to see these words come to life as you *model* them for her. Your daughter needs to observe the trait that you want her to replicate being put into action. You have to go first. The old saying "do as I say, not as I do" just won't cut it when it comes to the deepest core values we desire to instill. And not to mention, it's a ridiculous saying anyway.

Now, before you stop breathing or put this book down in dismay, you don't need to model *all* these traits *all* the time. You couldn't humanly do it. Instead, become intentional about a few of them at a time.

So, for example, today I'm choosing to model courage for my daughters. I model by doing and being—not just with words. Our tendency is to use our words to tell our daughters what they "should" be. Modeling how they *could* be is far more effective.

So, how could I model courage today? Perhaps it's trying a new food, talking to a stranger at the store, signing up for a new class, or doing something outside of my normal comfort zone.

Stop and think about that for a moment. How well has it worked for you when someone told you what they thought you should be or should do?

If we are anything alike, such a remark probably brought on shame—the feeling that I'm not good enough the way that I am, or guilt; that I wasn't doing things right. The last thing I want to do is to bring more shame and guilt on my daughters. The way the world works, they'll have plenty of their own to deal with in time.

In the past I was notorious for saying things to myself like, "I should be more like... I should be exercising more... I should be reading more..." One of my favorite coaches, Debbie, would say to me, "Alyce, stop 'should-ing' all over yourself!" Do you "should" all over yourself, too, Mom?

That's exactly what I did to myself. I was "should-ing" all over myself. And if it was okay for me to do that to myself, what was I giving permission to my daughters to do? And so the cycle begins.

But here's the good news. If I can model "should-ing," surely I can model other things as well. Our daughters will emulate, even subconsciously, what they see us do. This means I need to be conscious of what I'm choosing to model.

Model who you want to be for your daughter. Who do you envision your daughter being in the future? Who do you want to be? How do you want to show up in the world?

How about modeling compassion, kindness, self-care, a strong work ethic, perseverance, spontaneity, forgiveness, creativity, leadership, critical thinking, tenacity? The list is endless.

We want our daughters to be happy. So, what if we modeled it for them? It's never too late to live a life you love so you can show your daughter how to do it too.

We say we are willing to die for our daughters, but are we willing to live fully so they can too? Know that you can choose at any moment to be whoever you want to be. Choose who you want to be. And choose what you want to model.

WHO ARE YOUR MODELS, MOM?
One of the greatest hacks to being the mom we want to be is by identifying models for ourselves to emulate. "Who is already modeling the kind of mom I want to be?" Success will always leave clues. We don't need to reinvent the wheel in anything. We just need to find the models we wish to adopt and copy them. Once you copy them, you can adapt to make it your own.

I've picked up mothering models from women I've met at church, in business circles, in the school pick-up line, through books and podcasts, conferences and seminars, and so many more. Models are absolutely everywhere if we're looking for them. We will always find what we are looking for, which is why where we choose to place our focus is so important. We can either choose our models to get more predictable results or allow fate to be our guide.

In the following chapters, we'll be looking at three areas where I've chosen to invest heavily in terms of modeling: mindset, leadership, and goals. Who we choose to model in these areas and how we choose to show up as models for our girls matters. Raising entrepreneurial-spirited daughters starts with how *we* choose to live our lives as moms. The entrepreneurial spirit requires taking some risks that can help us live more fulfilling lives and which will ultimately lead to our daughters seeing firsthand how to do the same.

It's never too late to live a life you love—and in turn, to model for your daughter how to have the resourcefulness to do the same.

CHAPTER TWO

Mindset

"What you do makes a difference, and you have to decide what kind of difference you want to make."

—JANE GOODALL

When my girls were little (eight, six, three, and newborn), people would nostalgically tell me that the "days are long and the years are short." I wanted to strangle them because the days seemed to go by in football minutes. Excruciatingly long, exhausting, drawn-out, never-ending days. Eating a cold, crusty bagel or brushing my teeth felt like luxuries. Success was just survival and making it through another day.

I ran my days in a state of constant exhaustion. I continued to work full time outside the home throughout, and outside of work, my days were filled with daycare and school drop-offs, packing lunches and bottles of formula, after school activities, birthday parties, sports, lessons, and deciding if we were having pizza or chicken nuggets for dinner. I came home after work to tidy up the kitchen so it was clean enough to eat. The idea of getting eight hours of sleep was but a dream. My goal was simply to survive. And my mind felt like literal mush. I could tangibly feel the loss of brain cells with each passing day. I felt fortunate to even have my head stay screwed onto my body.

Even in the midst of survival, I knew I wanted to somehow thrive. Survival felt so awful. I constantly felt like a Maryland blue crab trying to climb out of a bucket, only to see the blue sky and be pulled back down to the bottom.

I knew I wasn't willing to settle for average. And I know you aren't willing to settle either. The good news is that it only takes one person to change your life—you.

MINDSET MATTERS
In order to get yourself healthy, you need to rein in your mental and emotional health. I had been living a life where it felt like everything was running me instead of me running everything. I felt like I was experiencing an identity crisis. My days were filled with caring for others, and I felt hopelessly lost, desperately wanting to know myself again. I chose to become a student of myself so I could raise my girls well. They deserved to have a fully present and functioning mom—and so does your daughter.

Self-mastery is the way in which we gain clarity about what matters most to us so we can make decisions accordingly. If all of life is about making a series of decisions, knowing ourselves is key. Self-mastery is being in control of the ways we think, feel, and act. The alternative is living in victimhood and having life continually happening to us instead of life happening for us.

One battle we will each fight until the day we take our final breath is the battle that happens in our minds. Our thoughts are the first domino in a sequence of events:

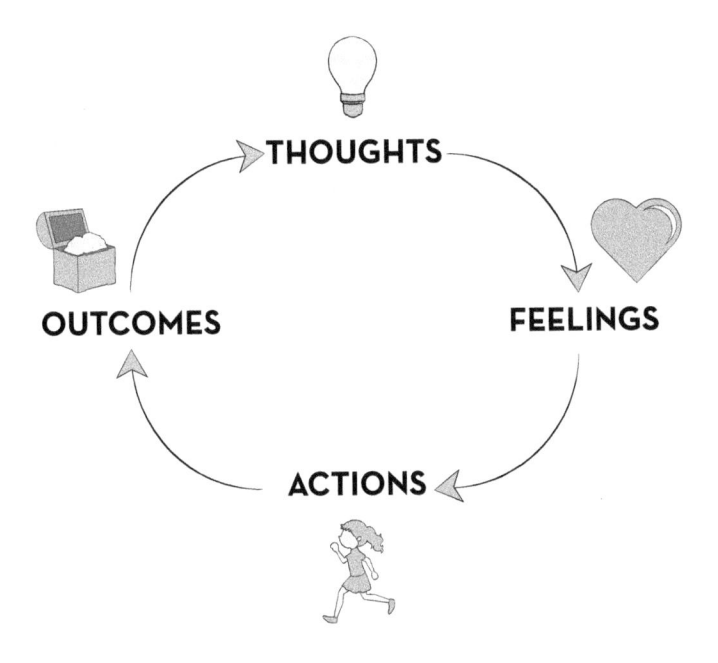

THOUGHTS → FEELINGS → ACTIONS → OUTCOMES → THOUGHTS

Our thoughts run our lives—on the conscious and subconscious levels. As Craig Groeschel says, "Our lives are always moving in the direction of our strongest thought." If our thoughts run our lives, we need to get a hold of them so they take us where we want to go.

Our brain, where our thoughts are generated, is much like that of a computer. The internal wiring makes the system work. If the brain is producing favorable thoughts or beliefs, we don't usually pay much attention. If we're experiencing results or outcomes that are unfavorable, we have the ability to make some changes to our programming in order to change the whole story. Change is possible. This is good news for those who don't like where they are.

What are some thoughts or beliefs you hold about yourself that are not currently serving you?

Here were some of mine:

- I'm not smart enough.
- I'm not pretty enough.
- I'm not thin enough.
- I'm not as good of a mom because I work outside the home.
- My girls will be malnourished because I'm a bad cook.
- I'm not athletic enough.
- If I don't put my daughter in this extracurricular activity, she won't be able to do/become/have…

What are some thoughts or beliefs you hold about raising a daughter? What thoughts do you hold deep down that aren't serving you? The mindset with which we come into momhood has a direct correlation to the daughters we raise.

Here are some of the things I used to believe about being a girl mom:

- Girls are overly emotional.
- There will always be drama with girls.
- Girls are only easy to raise when they are little.

- Girls are harder to raise as teenagers than boys.
- Just lock up your teenage girl and let her out when she's an adult.
- Girls are jealous of one another.
- Sibling rivalry is real.
- Girls will cost you a fortune.

But what if these things aren't actually rock-solid truths? What if we can change these thoughts so we have a different outcome? There is a way to create the reality you want to have because your chosen thoughts and mindset *will* create your reality. Since you will always find what you are looking for, it is vital to make sure your mindset matches the outcome you want to have. You can change the story at any time simply because you are writing it!

When our second daughter was born and came home from the hospital, we heard from multiple sources, "Watch out for that sibling rivalry!" We didn't know any better, so we believed it. And, sure enough, we actually found ways to prove this statement true. We were unknowingly on hyper alert, expecting her older sister to be jealous of how we were giving attention to the new baby.

But something happened a few months in that caused me to change my thinking.

I was putting the baby to bed, and Karissa (older sister) asked if she could help. She sat with Lorra and just loved on her. The thought suddenly occurred to me, *If I believed sibling rivalry didn't exist, how would I, myself, show up differently? And if I did, would the outcome be different?*

Two creation points are involved when forming our chosen mindsets. The first creation point happens in our mind where we have to see our desired results first in our imagination. This creation could be a visualization or a written narrative that we journal. What things do you dream for your relationship with your daughter?

- My daughter is intelligent, strong, and smart.
- She is generous and compassionate.
- She loves her siblings.
- We have an open and authentic relationship that allows us to talk about and through hard things.
- She is the master of her emotions.

All of these statements are thoughts I have to create first in my mind before they can ever be produced in the physical world.

Consider Disney World, for example. Walt had to create the world in his mind first and get it on paper before it could ever be produced in the real physical world. And I'm sure most people thought he was nuts for even imagining it in the first place! Can you envision him saying to his brother, "Hey, Roy! Let's buy up thousands of acres of Florida swamp land and build a fictitious world of flying elephants, giant castles, talking mice, princesses, and parades! It will be amazing. I promise!"

No different here with raising girls. People will certainly think you're crazy too.

The second creation point is using words to have the desired results show up in the world. How do you have a daughter who joyfully welcomes her sibling into the world? You start speaking it into existence with your words. You tell her what it will be like. You paint the picture as if it's already real and happening.

How do you create the open and authentic relationship? You create it first in your mind, and then you model it with her in the physical realm through words and actions.

If you're not sure where to start, think back to what your childhood was like. What do you wish you had at your daughter's age? Be all of the things you wish you had then. Give your daughter all the things you wish you had—not in the material sense but rather in the emotional realm.

> *The greatest gifts you can give your daughter come from the places of pain you've experienced in your own childhood.*

In raising my girls, I knew I wanted them to be strong, independent thinkers. Strong, independent thinkers don't just happen by accident. It's a skill that can be taught, developed, and modeled. As a young parent, I started watching for ways other moms were exposing their daughters to bigger ways of thinking.

I started to picture in my mind the kinds of experiences I wanted our girls to have. I imagined them coming to events with us where we could learn and grow together. I pictured them loving to learn and loving to read. I pictured them loving travel and enjoying music. As I created these vivid images in my mind, my actions subconsciously lined up with the vision. We started bringing the girls with us to personal growth events when they were as young as seven years old. We chose to financially invest in taking them to conferences where they would hear world-class speakers give inspirational talks.

As we started to dive into growing ourselves personally, our journey led us to Tony Robbins. My husband and I attended one of his popular Unleash the Power Within events, which is widely known for the fire walk. Every participant has the opportunity to walk barefoot across a bed of hot coals. The practice goes as far back as 1200 BC in a variety of cultures and from various parts of the world.

I was anxious and a bit fearful of the fire walk. Most people assume it happens on the last day of the four-day event, when it actually happens on day one! But really, why in the world would anyone in their right mind willingly choose to walk on burning hot coals?

The whole lesson is around our mindset and the power of mind over matter. I visualized over and over in my mind successfully completing the fire walk unharmed and victorious. I visualized going home to tell the girls that Mom did it! I visualized myself taking a picture in front of the "Firewalker!" sign in the lobby. I imagined the incredible high I would feel as a result of accomplishing something so wild and crazy!

Conquering the fire walk was far more than the victory of just completing the task. It was a realization that I could create outcomes in my mind that didn't previously exist and make them a reality. It was a demonstration of how powerful our minds actually are.

And you know what I started thinking about after I completed the fire walk? I started thinking, *I wonder how soon our girls would be ready for this experience?* Some think it's crazy, yet I knew we wanted strong, independent young women. If they could grasp this concept at a young age, what might be possible for their future?

Our oldest daughter, Karissa, went to the event at fourteen years old. She was excited at first, but her enthusiasm turned into complete fear as the evening wore on and the reality of what was about to happen set in. My husband made it clear that she didn't have to do the fire walk, but she did have to walk up with him and he would find someone to help her get back without participating.

When she and Seth approached the front of the line, Seth asked one of the leaders to help her as promised. Seth did the fire walk himself, and when he reached the other side, the Tony Robbins trainer who was with Karissa told him to keep going and that she was okay. So he proceeded to wait for her back at their seats in the convention center.

Over an hour passed. Then two. He didn't know where she was, but the environment was a trusted one, and he knew she'd be well cared for by the trainer.

When Karissa walked in, she was beaming from ear to ear. She hadn't just done the fire walk once—but twice! The trainer told her she didn't have to do the walk. She simply had to look into people's eyes as they approached the fire walk, and she had to decide if the person was in the right state of mind to go. The trainer knew that if Karissa could see in others what it took to be ready, she could create it in her mind for herself, which is exactly what happened.

Karissa was there until the end of the fire walk when the crew who work the event also get to participate. A member of the crew made Karissa an honorary member and asked her to join them. She said yes and joyfully completed it a second time! One of my favorite pictures is of Seth and Karissa standing in front of the firewalker sign with Seth holding up one finger and Karissa holding up two—to signify how many times each of them had walked on fire that night.

Once you walk on fire at fourteen (twice in this case), what can you *not* do in life? Karissa's mindset was deeply shifted in those moments, and that shift has impacted how she has shown up in the world ever since.

Our second daughter, Lorra, went to the same firewalking event at age twelve and again at fourteen. Our third daughter, Annika, completed the fire walk at age twelve. And our youngest is currently ten, so she's waiting for her turn!

Your mindset matters. The good news is that you are fully in control of it. The bad news is that the world won't support your positive mindset. In fact, it will constantly bombard you with messages of fear, inadequacy, and shame. It's one of the reasons we stopped watching television years ago. Little did we know the screens would end up in our hands in the form of a phone. Negative messaging is everywhere (hello, social media), which makes it infinitely more of a battle to capture our thoughts every day. We may not have control of our first thought, but we can always control the second one.

Modeling mindset is one of the most important things you'll ever do for yourself and for your daughter. It won't happen by accident, but rather, it requires purposeful intention. It becomes even more powerful when created in community with others. The possibilities are endless when you understand the power your mindset has over your outcomes. Don't leave your life's direction to chance. It only takes one person to change your life by way of your thoughts—you.

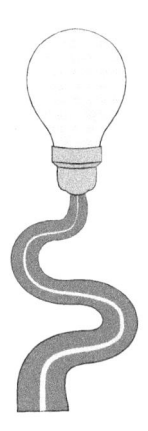

THE PATH TO MAGIC:
1. What does the phrase "mind over matter" mean to me?

2. How is my mindset helping (or hindering) a particular situation or activity of my life?

3. How could I expand my mindset to create a new opportunity for myself? For my daughter?

4. Imagine mom/daughter dates at various stages and seasons of life. What do I want them to look like?

CHAPTER THREE

Lead

"Leadership is about making others better as a result of your presence and making sure that impact lasts in your absence."
—SHERYL SANDBERG

When Lorra was eleven, we walked into Five Below, and she noticed a little wall hanging that said,

"Life Is Short. Buy the Dress."

She looked at it for a few seconds and said, "That's dumb. It should say, 'Life is short. Own the company that makes the dress,' and that way you could have both."

She just moved on and went to look at another shiny object that caught her attention.

But I stopped cold in my tracks. *What just happened? I thought. How did her brain go there so quickly and effortlessly?* The thought she just spit out in passing was one that would never have crossed my mind naturally. How did she connect the dots from buying a dress to owning the company that makes the dress? She was thinking bigger than I was, and I was quietly impressed.

Long after we left the store, I couldn't help but wonder if her thinking was innate or if it was possibly something we had fostered that allowed her to think that way? What had she seen modeled elsewhere that gave her the framework to begin thinking differently?

Because she had been exposed to models of entrepreneurship, she didn't start with the assumption of working for someone else. Instead, she saw the opportunity in being the owner and leading the way. When Lorra turned sixteen and got her driver's license, one of the first things she did was to start applying for jobs. This seemed like an interesting choice for a budding entrepreneur. She was diligent about finding a place that aligned with her school schedule and passion for health, so she looked into local juice shops. After landing one that fit her schedule, I asked her why she chose to get a job if she planned to start her business soon. She simply answered that she wanted to at least have the experience of working for someone else—once.

It's easy to look at someone like her and say she's a "born leader."

Are leaders born or made? I've heard that question asked many times before, and I believe it's the wrong question. The question presupposes that some people are leaders and some are not.

Yet if we look at, what I believe to be, the most powerful definition of leadership from leadership expert, Dr. John Maxwell, it says:

Leadership is influence.

Influence. Nothing more and nothing less. If this is true, it means we are all leaders. Every one of us holds some level of influence, whether for good or for bad, and in varying degrees. What makes us all different is in how and with whom we use that influence.

Mom, you have incredible influence, and that means you are a leader. Regardless of whether you lead people outside of your home, in the work place, or in a volunteer role, you are a leader to your daughter, as you influence her more than any human being on the planet—at least for many significant years. Even if you never thought yourself to be a leader before, you certainly became one once you took on the title of "Mom."

So where did you go to leadership school? Who taught you to be a leader? For many of us the answer is nothing more than a blank stare. We simply unconsciously modeled what we observed growing up, or we parent in a way directly contrary to what was modeled for us and hope for the best. For most moms, little intention, if any, is given to how to lead at home. But that's not who you are, Mom—or you wouldn't be reading this book.

Other cultures and societies around the world understand the power women—mothers in particular—have within a community. During a trip I took with fourteen American women to the Democratic Republic of Congo (DRC), we went to hear stories of women who had experienced first-hand violence. Women who had been brutally assaulted in the harshest of ways. Women of all ages were targets—not just the adults. Sitting there listening to these women as a privileged American woman and mother, I was angry, sad, and confused. Why were these women and young girls such targets?

Two of the women on the trip, Belinda Bauman and Lynne Hybels, were well-versed in the DRC conflict. Belinda is the founder of an organization called One Million Thumbprints, which helps women affected by violence in war zones. Lynne has traveled to Africa countless times and advocates on behalf of women in these dire situations. They shared with me the pattern they have observed in countries such as the DRC. In order to break the communities and ultimately the infrastructure of an entire country, all that had to be done was to break the women. And, as Lynne reminded us, those looking to destroy the women believed that "it is cheaper to rape a woman than to waste a bullet."

Because these women in the DRC led their children and families and ran businesses, they became the target. Their leadership and influence is the very glue that holds the society together. Mom, you are a part of the very same fabric. Together, we unite our family, our neighborhoods, our communities, our states, and our country. You have leadership and influence far beyond what you realize.

LEAD YOURSELF FIRST

Once you own the identity of a leader, the next question is, "Who do I lead first?"

Take a look in the mirror and start right there. You are the hardest person you'll ever have the privilege of leading.

You are the CEO of your life. You have the ability and power to control your own resources. The CEO of a company oversees all components of a business. The CEO determines the vision, goals, and plan to achieve and grow. So what does it mean to be the CEO of your own life?

As CEO of your life, you determine the path toward success. No one else can or will accept that responsibility. Sadly, however, many women never assume this role or identity. Instead, they wander through life much like aiming a bowling ball while blindfolded, hoping it hits a pin instead of ending up in the gutter.

We've never lived in a time in history where leadership tools and resources have been so accessible and abundant. As the CEO of your life, you have the power to make the choices to bring about the change you want to see. If you want to learn a new skill, education can be found in a book, podcast, or YouTube video. If you want more time, you can choose to eliminate things from your schedule. You can choose what time to go to bed or wake up. If you want more energy, you can choose how to fuel your body with nutrients or take care of it through exercise. If you don't like your present vocation, where you live, or how much money you make, you single handedly have the ability to change them all.

I know I won't always love everything about my life. But I also know I have the ability to make choices and bring more of what I want into my life rather than allowing life to just pass me by.

You are the CEO of your own life. Sometime you just need a reminder so you can act like it. However, many people begin leading their own lives only after they get a second chance—possibly after a health scare or the passing of a close friend or relative.

Do you know you have two lives? Your second life begins the moment you realize you only have one.

This second chance, or wake-up call, is sometimes referred to as a mid-life crisis. Instead of the term "crisis," I believe it's an awakening. A "waking up" to your own life. Awakening to the realization that most of us have been sleepwalking through life instead of living with purpose and direction.

Sleepwalking through life is a tricky thing. It can be hard to realize that one is doing it. In retrospect, I now realize I was sleepwalking for the majority of my life even though I was doing really great things—productive things, world-changing things. Yet I was asleep. I was subconsciously following a prewritten script instead of actively leading my own life.

For many women, this happens around age forty, or at what author Bob Buford refers to as "halftime." When I realized I had been sleepwalking through life, I started to imagine what I could do if I was fully awake and alive with my eyes wide open.

The last few years have largely been about "waking up" for me. I'm still waking up, and I still fight the desire to go back to sleep, metaphorically speaking, because sometimes leading your own life feels hard. There is no road map when you travel down unpaved, unmarked roads. It's often bumpy, dark, and unpredictable. Leading requires vision, goal-setting, and planning. Going through life asleep—the path of least resistance—is easy and natural for most of us. We go along doing all of the "shoulds" of life.

- "I should go to college."
- "I should get a good job."
- "I should buy a house."
- "I should get married."
- "I should have a baby."

And then what?

If you don't have clear direction and purpose for your own life, you'll be living someone else's plans for you. And as the late business philosopher Jim Rohn said, "If you live someone else's plans, do you know what they have planned for you? Not much."

Are you okay settling for "not much"?

Me neither.

Some days I still catch myself asleep to my own life, but those days are becoming fewer and farther between. I'm fighting habits of years of doing all the things I thought I "should" do and spending more time thinking about doing "what's *mine* to do." I have to constantly remind myself that I'm running my own race at my own pace. And you're running yours. Sometimes I get confused and caught up in comparison and veer off and bump into you in your lane. Please forgive me in advance. I'm working on that. It's part of leading myself first that I come back to often.

If you want to build a life you love with intention and purpose, it all starts with building and leading yourself. Build, create, and become the person you love most, and the life you love will follow.

LEAD YOUR DAUGHTER SECOND
It feels counterintuitive to lead our daughter second. We have a natural motherly instinct to do anything and everything for her first, which is why the analogy from the airlines of putting your own oxygen mask on continues to be a poignant one. You cannot take care of others if you are not healthy yourself. Put your own oxygen mask on first and breathe deeply. Then help your daughter. If we want to model healthy leadership, we need to show our daughters that putting on our own oxygen mask first is the path to helping more people. And sometimes it will feel counterintuitive and selfish.

As I started waking up to my own life, I looked at the roles I play in the world and which ones were unique to me. I was actually quite startled to see that I was pretty much replaceable in most roles in my life. I was equally startled to see only *one* real role was uniquely mine.

Mom.

A significant purpose of my life is to lead my daughters. To be a model for them. To lead them to other models in various areas of life.

Leading your daughter without leading yourself first is downright impossible. Do you know what we call those who choose to "lead" by telling others what to do? Dictators. And if you're reading this book, I know that's not the kind of mom you aspire to be.

Since it is downright impossible to lead my daughters without leading myself first, my initial priority became clear: Become the CEO of my life. And, whether this is a new idea or merely one that needs a tune-up, becoming your own CEO may be your priority too.

THE PATH TO MAGIC
1. In what areas of life do I lead (influence) with confidence?

2. Which people in my world do I influence? Who most influences me?

3. On a scale of one to ten, how well am I leading myself? How well am I leading my daughter?

4. In what ways am I leading my life well? (Don't be shy here!)

5. How can I help my daughter adopt being a leader as a part of her identity?

CHAPTER FOUR

Goals

―

"Would you tell me, please, which way I ought to go from here?" Alice asked the Cheshire Cat.

"That depends a good deal on where you want to get to," said the Cat.

"I don't much care where," said Alice.

"Then it doesn't matter which way you go," said the Cat.
—LEWIS CARROLL, ALICE'S ADVENTURES IN WONDERLAND

Imagine the view from 19,341 feet. That's the height of Mount Kilimanjaro in Tanzania.

When was the last time you did something for the first time? When was the last time you did something really hard for you? Maybe it wasn't something that you perceive as hard for others, but something that for you was a real challenge? I took on one of these challenges in 2016. I was feeling bored and a little (or a lot) burned out from life. A client of mine, Belinda, who quickly turned into a lifelong friend and sister, sent me a late-night email that simply said, "Would you think about doing this with me?" And she included a picture of Kilimanjaro, the tallest freestanding mountain in all of Africa.

Now, to give you some context, camping for me up to this point meant a crusty motel. You know, one of those rooms where you won't even take off your socks because the carpet is just that… interesting. One of those places that would have had the vibrating beds if you put in a quarter in the 1980s. That, to me, *was* camping.

But the idea wasn't to climb Kilimanjaro just for the fun of the adventure or for the accolades. We were going as a group of fourteen women, ages twenty-two to sixty-five, to raise money and awareness for women who have been affected by violence in war zones, such as Syria, Sudan, the Democratic Republic of Congo, and Rwanda. We didn't all know each other beforehand, but we were connected by the common thread of our ringleader, Belinda.

The primary goal was threefold:

- To hear first-hand stories from women affected by violence and to understand the issues more fully to raise awareness
- To raise $250,000 for grassroots programs to support these women
- For all fourteen of us to reach the summit of Kilimanjaro and return home safely

Though many people climb Kilimanjaro for sport and for the challenge of conquering one of the world's "Seven Summits," that wasn't important to us. We were a pretty unlikely group to be climbing a mountain when you looked at us collectively! We were composed of students, authors, housewives, Realtors, business owners, nonprofit leaders, artists, and gender-based violence activists, to name a few. There have been numerous athletes and physical fitness junkies who didn't make it to the top of Mt. Kilimanjaro. You only tend to hear the stories of those who did make it. When we were in Africa, however, we heard the stories of names you would know who didn't make it to the top.

So how could an unlikely group of women of all shapes, sizes, backgrounds, abilities, and ages all make it?

We understood our goal and had a plan to accomplish it. Goals come in all shapes and sizes, and this one was a tall order with lots of moving parts and people. Regardless of the size or scope, however, we can break down goals pretty simply.

Having a clearly stated goal is key. A great framework to setting goals is the "SMART" test. Goals must be:

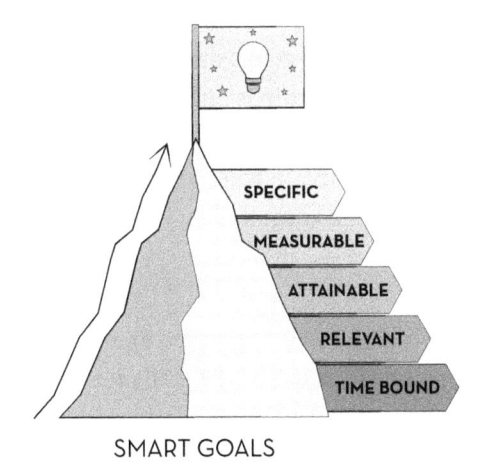

SMART GOALS

In a study conducted by Professor Gail Matthews, a psychologist from the Dominican University of California, research found those who simply wrote down their goals were 20 percent more likely to accomplish them than those who only thought about their goal. Additionally, those who set corresponding actions to their goals along with weekly peer accountability were 40 percent more likely to achieve their goals.

Thinking about your goal engages the right side of our brain, which includes the imaginative creative center. When we engage the logical left side of our brain through putting pen to paper, we engage our entire nervous system in the process, which leads to greater results.

The lesson? Write it down. Make it happen.

YOUR GOAL IS YOUR TICKET
We are either growing or we are dying at *all* times. There is no such thing as staying in place and just maintaining. It's simply an illusion. Setting a goal helps us get unstuck and back on to roads that lead to things and places we actually want.

A goal is your ticket to anywhere you want to go. It's your ticket to whoever you want to become. Goals allow you to thrive as opposed to survive.

Up until my early twenties, goals were more like checklists of things I knew I needed to do. The goals I had weren't necessarily inspiring or heart tugging in any way. I was probably afraid of failing, so I played it safe and turned ambitions more into a task list.

Things changed in 2001, however. For our first wedding anniversary, Seth and I went to downtown Chicago for the weekend as an escape from our suburban apartment. We booked a hotel on Priceline and explored the city. We sat in a Starbucks on Rush Street that weekend, and he pulled out a new journal. He said, "Let's a make a list of all of things we want to accomplish or do or have in the next year." I'd never done something like this before and was excited to see what we would come up with. It started as a to-do checklist. But when I ran out of those things, I was frustrated. I started to ask myself different questions at this point:

- Where do I want to travel?
- What do I want to see?
- Who do I want to visit?
- Who do I want to meet?
- How do I want to grow?
- Who do I want to hear in concert?
- What do I want to have?
- How do I want to invest?
- How do I want to contribute and give back?
- What do I want to do for fun?

Asking these questions started to open up so many more goals and dreams inside of me that I didn't even know were there. I felt a rush of adrenaline and childlike wonder flood my body. It felt *so good* to dream again! I had forgotten what it was like after the chores, routines, and pressures of real life had squashed this part of me into a small corner.

Some of the things that made my list were:

- Buying our first home
- Buying an investment property
- Visiting a friend in France
- Visiting a friend in Taiwan
- Taking flying lessons
- Giving 10 percent of our income to our church
- Getting a new designation in my field
- Singing the national anthem at a ball park
- Going to Montana
- Saving $20,000

These were really big things for my twenty-three-year-old self. I just challenged myself to keep adding to the list. The more I did it, the more addictive and fun it became and the less afraid I was of writing something bigger that seemed more outlandish. When I stopped thinking about "how" I would accomplish the goal and just kept writing things that would be cool to do, see, or have, I removed the limits from what was possible.

- Wouldn't it be cool to fly first class?
- Wouldn't it be cool to run a marathon?
- Wouldn't it be cool to get scuba certified?
- Wouldn't it be cool to go to Tahiti?
- Wouldn't it be cool to see U2 in concert?
- Wouldn't it be cool to write a $10,000 check to my favorite charity?
- Wouldn't it be cool to have a personal shopper at Nordstrom?
- Wouldn't it be cool to have a personal chef?

- Wouldn't it be cool to go on a safari in Africa?

Once I started, it was hard to stop, and I couldn't believe it. Just the exercise of writing down dreams was exhilarating. We continued to write down things throughout our fun weekend away.

And then on Monday we went back to real life.

Back to the nine-to-five grind for me in human resource management and Seth to being a certified public accountant. We worked five days, lived for the weekends, and rinsed and repeated. His commute was over ninety minutes each way, and mine was forty minutes each way. It was almost like that fun anniversary weekend away never happened.

Fast forward a whole year to our second anniversary. Being the creatures of habit we are (and due to our budget constraints), we decided to do the exact same thing as the previous year. I found us a screaming deal on a Priceline hotel, and we went downtown.

As we were packing up to leave for our trip, Seth asked, "Where's that journal we wrote in last year?" I had no earthly idea. I didn't even remember which journal it was or what it looked like. I most definitely hadn't seen it, looked at it, opened it, or thought about it in the past 364 days. I didn't even remember what he was talking about when he first asked.

He ended up finding it on a bookshelf somewhere, and we went back to the same Starbucks on Rush Street in downtown

GOALS · 69

Chicago. We opened it up after not having looked at it even once in the past year.

That's when my jaw hit the floor.

The number of things that we had actually accomplished or things that were in process of happening were mind blowing. We had taken one trip to Taiwan and we had the trip to France planned. I had taken my classes for my human resources designation. We had booked time for a Montana trip. We had the money saved for a house down payment. We were giving 10 percent to our church.

Now, a number of things hadn't happened too. But the truth is this: If we hadn't written down all of these in the first place, there's a good chance *none* of them would have happened. So while I don't recommend losing the journal for a year and never looking at it, the advice of writing down your goals remains. There is power in allowing your subconscious to do some heavy lifting when it comes to reaching your goals. Your subconscious mind takes it very seriously when you write down aspirations. It starts working all possible angles, even while you're asleep, to make it happen.

So, where to start?

First, let's look at the different primary areas of your life with the LYFEwheel:

LYFEWheel

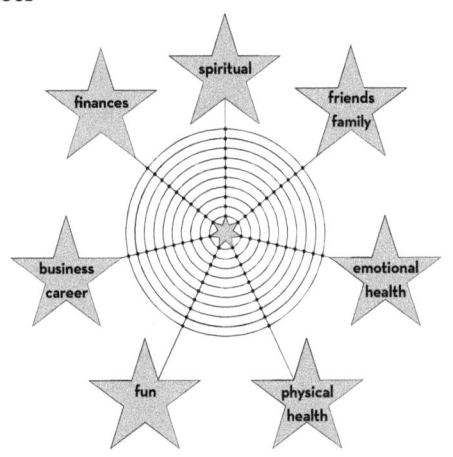

[Wheel diagram with eight stars labeled: spiritual, friends/family, emotional health, physical health, fun, business/career, finances, and a central star]

Grab a journal and start dreaming again. If you start writing goals in an area and get stuck, just move on until you find an area with least resistance. Find an environment that feels fun for you to be in while you start this exercise. It's a fun one because you can start, stop, and pick it back up at any time.

Don't be shy and don't hold back. If you think of it, write it down without judgment. It doesn't matter if it's something to accomplish in one week, one month, one year, or ten years. If you find your mind drifting to reasons why you can't do something, gently remind yourself that you don't need to know how. This whole exercise is about dreaming again, reigniting your soul, and tapping back into your heart.

Modeling goal setting and dreaming for our girls is vital.

We, as moms, dream big dreams *for* them. Yet the biggest gift we can give is to show the path to dream big dreams for themselves. The way they will learn how to do this is by watching you modeling and living it out right in front of them. Dreaming big dreams for yourself isn't selfish at all. It's modeling how you'd want them to live too.

Post your goals and dreams somewhere in your home where your daughters can see them too. Have her do the same. Talk about your goals and dreams together. And watch the MAGIC happen.

THE PATH TO MAGIC

1. Imagine a day five years from now. We run into each other and meet for coffee. You start to tell me about how the past five years have been the best of your life! What high-point moments have happened in those five years that made them so amazing?

2. What environments make me feel most alive? (These are my best dream/goal writing spaces.)

3. What habit can I build into my schedule so I check in with my goals regularly?

4. Who are the people I want in my life to hold me accountable to, and celebrate the accomplishments of, my goals and dreams?

PART TWO:

AFFIRM

"What people think about you is not important. What you think about yourself means everything."

—UNKNOWN

An old Native American proverb speaks to the importance of our self-talk:

One evening, an elderly Cherokee told his grandson about a battle that goes on inside each of us.

He said, "My son, the battle is between two wolves inside us all. One is evil. It is anger, envy, jealousy, sorrow, regret, greed, arrogance, self-pity, guilt, resentment, inferiority, lies, false pride, superiority, and ego.

"The other is good. It is joy, peace, love, hope, serenity, humility, kindness, benevolence, empathy, generosity, truth, compassion, and faith.

"The same fight is going on inside you—and inside every other person too."

The grandson thought about it for a minute and then asked his grandfather, "Which wolf wins?"

The old Cherokee simply replied, "The one you feed."

How we feed ourselves and our daughters through words matters. How do you know if someone needs your grace, kindness, and words of encouragement? Because they're alive. Because they're breathing. We all need it. And if we all need it constantly, what a beautiful and life-giving skill to develop in ourselves and our daughters.

Learning to affirm yourself is just like working a muscle. Working out your "affirmation muscle" will surely make it stronger, just as lifting weights at the gym does for our physical bodies. And in order to affirm your daughter, you need to become pretty great at affirming yourself. All of humankind, us and daughters included, are just like houseplants who need water and sunlight. We just have way more emotions than the houseplants!

Each one of us has that voice in our head that just won't shut up. It's talking to us nonstop, even subconsciously when we are seemingly quiet. You know which voice I'm talking about, don't you? The running commentary that seems to have a mind of its own that just won't quit. It's what is known as our "self-talk."

Which wolf within yourself do you tend to feed most often? This is evident in the ways in which we talk to ourselves. I've caught myself saying things at times like:

- "How could you be so dumb?"
- "What a stupid mistake."
- "No one would ever want to be my friend."
- "This is too hard for me."
- "I should just quit."
- "I'm not good at anything."

If another human being talked to our daughter this way, we wouldn't allow it. So why do we allow our own inner voice to speak so harshly to us in this manner? If this underlying commentary is actually feeding our subconscious, which drives our behavior, it's critical that we make some changes.

Sometimes, we just need to stop listening and learn how to talk to ourselves instead.

THE TELEPHONE POLE

When I attended a Tony Robbins event called Life and Health Mastery a few years ago, the first day started on a beautiful Florida beach on Marco Island. It was relaxing, gorgeous, and peaceful. And in the distance, I could see forty-foot telephone poles rising above the pristine, gorgeous sand.

On the first day, and with only an hour of instruction, we were directed over to the telephone poles. One by one we put on a harness and took our turn climbing to the top. Once at the top, we had to stand straight up with nothing to hold on to. They told us to look around and enjoy the view, but my heart was beating out of my chest at this point, and it was a bit hard to enjoy anything.

And then? We were supposed to jump. I just had to trust that the little guy on the ground who controlled the pulley system on my harness wasn't going to let me fall to my death. No biggie.

For some of you, this would be game on! For me? Not so much. I've been quite unfond of heights from a young age and really hate the feeling of falling.

The T-shirt I wore that day was chosen on purpose. I picked a shirt representing one of my favorite nonprofits, Believe Big. It's a gray shirt with bright yellow letters. I knew I had to "believe big" to do this thing of which I was terrified. My teammates on the ground were cheering me on and encouraging and affirming me loudly, though it sounded faint from the top of the pole. A million voices inside my own head were screaming loudly as well. I don't pretend to know the diameter of the pole I was standing on, but at that moment, it felt like it was twelve inches. One wrong move and I would be off the edge.

I remember I was up there for a long time, though I couldn't tell you how long. Long enough that Seth had to edit his video recording down. At some point (I have zero recollection of when I made the decision), I jumped. I didn't die. And I was so incredibly proud of myself. My heart continued to race for quite some time after as we went into a debrief session about what we experienced.

During the debrief, I was able to verbalize within our little community what happened when I chose to jump:

"Instead of listening to myself, I started talking to myself. Loudly."

I literally started screaming *to* myself and *at* myself as I was standing at the top of the pole. I needed my own affirming voice to be louder than anything else around me.

Sometimes we need to borrow other people's belief in us until ours has the chance to catch up. In this case, I needed the belief of others *and* I also needed a pep talk from myself. I needed my community to affirm that I could do it and I needed me to affirm and believe in myself.

Talking to yourself is a part of building the critical muscle. By choosing to talk loudly to myself despite how I felt (it can feel weird, uncomfortable, or downright cheesy), I was exercising the muscle. I needed to affirm myself as much as I needed others around me, cheering me on. I needed to use my own voice to talk to myself. Sometimes, it's all we have. But in most cases, it's all we need.

What is an affirmation?

Affirmations are statements designed to create change within oneself. They are the stories we tell about ourselves—to ourselves. They can be inspirational or can redirect our focus to goals we have set for ourselves. The subconscious mind internalizes our affirmations and gets to work on making them come to fruition. As my friend, Tami, taught me years ago, "the subconscious can't take a joke!" That's why it's vitally important that the words we speak to ourselves be ones that are empowering and life giving.

Affirmations exercise your brain, strengthening it to become the way you want it to be. The word affirmation itself comes from the Latin word *affirmare*, which means "to make steady, strengthen."

Word affirmations are composed of three simple parts.

1. Affirmations are in the first person to be most effective and compelling.
2. Affirmations are positive statements.
3. Affirmations evoke a positive emotion.

By repeating, both internally and aloud, purposefully chosen phrases, we are giving strength to the thoughts we want to think about ourselves.

- "I am courageous and brave."
- "I am focused and optimistic."
- "I am worthy of living a life I love."
- "I have all the resources I need."
- "I am always learning and growing."
- "I am grateful for my health and wellbeing."

I wish there was a class in school that taught us how to talk to ourselves. I graduated from college with an undergraduate degree in communications, yet no one ever taught me how to talk to myself. How we talk to ourselves is undeniably tied to how we talk to others, so it's most certainly worth the effort to learn. We can only give others what we have, so modeling affirmations is vital in how we talk to ourselves and in how we talk to our girls.

Research from MRI evidence suggests that practicing self-affirmations can stimulate and increase neural pathways. Our words actually have the ability to heal our mind and body. Words are incredibly powerful tools that can give life or bring death (Cascio, 2016).

Neuroplasticity is the ability of the brain to continue growing and evolving in response to life experiences. The brain can actually change and grow over time by creating new neurons and building new networks. It was once believed that the brain was set in its ways after childhood, but, thankfully, we now know this isn't true. This is great news for all of us, for it means it is possible to change dysfunctional patterns of thinking and acting and to develop new ways of rationalizing, new mindsets, new skills, and new abilities (Psychology Today, 2022).

In these next chapters, we'll take a look at how our community, our values, and our willingness to risk our perceived safety directly relate to our ability to affirm ourselves and our daughters. How would your life look differently if you only fed the "good wolf"—the one that calls out the parts of you that dream big, live confidently, give generously, and empower others? The "good wolf" doesn't grow without some help from you, the surrounding community, and the willingness to take some risks. Ready to feed that "good wolf"? Let's do it together.

CHAPTER SIX

Community

"Friendship is born at that moment when one person says to another, 'You too? I thought I was the only one.'"
—C.S. LEWIS

Jessica was one of the main reasons I made it to the top of Kilimanjaro. Not because she was physically there with me, because she most definitely wasn't. She was a mere 7,697 miles away in Baltimore praying for us, but the day before I left for Africa, she insisted on driving forty minutes out of her way, with her two young kids in tow, to meet me at REI where I was buying last minute camping supplies. She wanted me to take her iPod that she had loaded with hours of encouraging music. I told her I didn't need her to do that and she didn't need to inconvenience herself to meet me. But she insisted. I was completely sure I wouldn't use it.

I met Jessica in my church youth group when I was fourteen. I never seemed to fit in with my age group as a kid, so I was invited in to a college Bible study. The younger sister of one the college students was also invited, and being only a year apart in age, Jessica and I became fast friends. She was homeschooled and had a different schooling experience than I did, but we shared a love of music and faith. During several years throughout college, we ended up more out of touch than not (remember, cell phones and email weren't a thing yet), but we reconnected again in our early twenties and were in each other's weddings. Today, we're closer than ever despite living thousands of miles apart. She's often my first call or text when I have a harebrained idea or thought. She's the first one there to pray for me when I need it. If we don't talk for weeks, and I call to ask for a favor, she jumps at the opportunity to help. Friends who can pick up right where we left off regardless of time that has passed are the best of kinds in my mind. She inspires me to grow. Jess will encourage me even when I don't think I need it (but really do). She finds the best in me and makes sure I bring it to the world.

On the summit night of our climb, we started at 11:00 p.m. to make it to the top by sunrise. I became separated from my group, and before long it was just me and my guide, who spoke no English, climbing together. It was dark and the loneliest void I have ever experienced. I could only see the next step in front of me, thanks to my little headlamp. The lights from the campsite were long gone. Looking up or around made me dizzy with what I imagine the start of vertigo must be like. The altitude made a single breath hard work. The sky was pitch black, and the stars were countless—but I couldn't stop to take any of it in. I was focused on breathing and taking one small, slow step at a time, finding a rhythm that would hopefully get me to my destination.

When I realized it was going to be this long, quiet, and lonely road with just me and my thoughts, I remembered the iPod. I threw in my headphones, and the David Crowder band songs carried me all the way through the darkest hours of the night until dawn—at least seven hours of climbing in the dark. The words of the songs were the way in which Jessica was affirming me and encouraging me forward while being half a world away.

How did she know? How did Jessica know I needed that iPod? She was a part of my village. She knew me at a deep level, and she knew how I was wired. We were a part of the same community and had lived life together. Jessica knew the way she could encourage and affirm me from the other side of the world would be through this gift of music. Her belief and faith in me was part of what carried me up the mountain in the darkest of times.

FUTURISTIC FIVE

Think about your closest friends. What are they like? What do they believe? What do they do vocationally? How do they spend their time? You can tell a lot about a person by the friends they keep. In fact,

We can predict the success of our daughters' futures by the friends they keep.

I secretly call my daughter's closest friends the "Futuristic Five." Show me your friends, and I'll show you your future. I heard this line from a mentor growing up so often I would roll my eyes at her. However, she couldn't have been more right.

We are the sum of the five people with whom we spend the most time. The "Futuristic Five" shape our beliefs and thoughts, which are what ultimately shape our actions and decisions.

One of my mentors, Gary Keller, the founder of Keller Williams Realty, told a story about how he didn't love his son's friends and the influence they were having on him. He was aware the choices made by the friends his son kept weren't leading him in a positive direction.

So what do you do in that case? Think of this like a choose your own adventure book...

- Tell your daughter she is required to find a new group of friends because you don't like them.
- Tell your daughter's friends directly you don't like them and ask them to stay away from your daughter.
- Find a way to influence your daughter's friends so that they all start to go in a different direction.
- Do nothing and hope for the best.

Truly—what would you do in this situation? Some of you have likely already been in this place. When your daughter is young, and if it's a kid in preschool, you may just choose to not have playdates together. It's a bit easier when they rely on you for food and transportation and don't have much of an opinion. But what about when they get older and her free will comes into play? Do you jeopardize your relationship with your daughter? Do you tell her your thoughts about the situation?

Gary Keller made an interesting choice. He knew that reading the right kinds of books would make an impact on all of the kids, his son included. So he decided to start paying them to read books that he chose.

Think about that. Incentivizing not just his son, but his son's friends, with twenty dollars to ingest books like *Think and Grow Rich*, *How to Win Friends and Influence People*, *The Richest Man in Babylon*, *Rich Dad, Poor Dad*, and more. You can find a list of must-read books for you and your daughter at www.TheMAGICMom.com.

Those kids were now excited to read! And as they took in the words, their beliefs and thinking began to change. As their beliefs and thinking changed, so did their actions. The Futuristic Five was looking better and better.

When Gary's son got married, his son's friends all thanked Gary for what he did when they were younger. They recognized that his influence changed the trajectory of their lives. What an incredible legacy he left, not only for his son, but for his son's Futuristic Five.

What will you do when this happens? Because chances are it will. Your daughter's community of friends will either bring her up or down. I promise you it won't be neutral. Do you know her tendencies? Does she lean toward being a follower or a leader in her friend groups?

Practically speaking, we've done several small things that you can begin today in order to affect your daughter's community. Start by hosting small groups of your daughter and her friends at your home. Invite them to watch a thought-provoking movie or documentary together and discuss it with them afterward. Set up the opportunity to create vision boards together. Encourage her sports team or church youth group to meet up at your home on a regular basis. One of our girls goes to a school where there are only twenty in the high school, so we've offered our backyard so they can have their own prom right here!

Wherever you find yourself, just start. You can influence her community and foster affirming, life-giving relationships as a result.

WHO IS IN YOUR VILLAGE?
Finding and making friends can be challenging at any age, especially if you skew toward the introverted side. Developing friendships and building community require vulnerability, authenticity, and loads of courage. It requires putting yourself out there with people to find connection points. Making friends and developing relationships is risky! We put ourselves in the position to be rejected, dismissed, and hurt. On the contrary, we also allow for the possibility of connecting with kindred spirits who make our souls come alive. Individuals crave community where we feel our most authentic selves and where we can use our natural gifts to ultimately benefit the whole.

Whereas our natural instinct is to impress people with areas where we are confident and strong, our ultimate goal, if it is connection with others, is best achieved through sharing our weaknesses, pain, and failures. We connect with others through our ugliest, most real selves—not through the dolled-up versions which we'd much rather they see.

Mom, find your community and your village first. Your daughter will be watching to see how you model friendships and community. If you find it valuable and life giving, so will she. If you go at life as a lone ranger, so will she. Life is far more enjoyable and so much easier to navigate with trusted friends along the way to come alongside you and cheer you on when you find yourself walking on the side of the mountain in the dark. Find people and communities that support your values and beliefs in how you want to raise your daughter. If you're in some communities currently that don't support how you want to raise her, find a new one. Sometimes communities end when life circumstances change or when you outgrow it. Just make sure you're never without one. We weren't made to do this life alone. We're weren't made to raise our daughters alone.

CREATE THE VILLAGE

Mom, you are a powerful force in helping to shape your daughter's community. Stack the deck in her favor. Introduce her to a variety of communities starting with ones like Girl Scouts, church youth groups, sports teams, theater groups, entrepreneurial clubs, or community service outreach groups. Go participate in activities with her. Serve at a soup kitchen, organize a group of moms and daughters to do a project together such as collecting canned goods for the local food pantry.

If the right community for your family doesn't exist, perhaps you're being called to create it.

When we moved to Austin we were fortunate enough to know a few families, and we just started extending invitations to people who seemed to share something in common with us—from the girls' school communities, church, real estate world, business owners, neighbors, and more. All you have to do is find one common thread. And sometimes the common thread is as simple as living in the same vicinity or enjoying a similar hobby or just the mere fact that we're all a bit lonely and in need of more connection.

Community begins when one person simply says to another, "I'm feeling a bit unsure and alone. Would it be okay if we do a little bit of life together?" Don't be surprised when you hear in response, "Really? I thought I was the only one."

THE PATH TO MAGIC

1. What gifts do I bring to a community? Brag on yourself here—toot your horn! What gifts does my daughter bring?

2. What kind of community am I wanting or needing to be a part of?

3. How can I create more opportunities for the kind of community I need? (Hint: If you need it, others do too)

4. Who is a great community builder whom I already know? What could I learn from her that would make a difference in how I participate in, or lead, a community?

5. Sometimes we have the right message for our daughter, but we aren't the right messenger. Someone in our village, however, could be. What intentions could you set today to ensure you're surrounded by other trusted "messengers"?

CHAPTER SEVEN

Values

"Your core values are the deeply held beliefs that authentically describe your soul."

—JOHN C. MAXWELL

I received a message on Facebook from a business owner asking if we could talk about having me become her coach. We hadn't ever talked before, but she had heard me speak at a conference the year prior. She then went on to google me and to find other places I had presented, and she heard me say these words:

"How can I be more me?"

It struck her so much that she wrote it down and put it on her office bulletin board so she can see it every day. I had no idea this was the case until we hopped on a Zoom call together and she mentioned it as the catalyst for wanting to connect.

So many of us—me included—get caught up in trying to be like someone else. I've attended countless real estate and business conferences where we put people on stages with accolades and undying praise. We hold them up as the gold standard for their achievements. Attendees see them as the examples and leave with their newfound heroes on pedestals. I did the same thing for years. I was inspired by their successes and made decisions about my life, family, and business based on what I saw in little snippets from a stage. I created a pretty great life and family using this strategy, but something still felt off.

I wouldn't figure it out until years later when I started developing personal friendships with many of the people who I had revered from afar.

The secret I learned?

Many of them didn't want to be themselves either.

So why had I been spending so much time, energy, and effort trying to be them if they didn't even want to be like themselves?

And then it hit me. I was merely emulating others because I wasn't clear on my own values. I was trying to latch on to someone else's values by default. And when we emulate someone else and their set of values, it's like a terrible photocopy—an illegible copy of a copy of a copy. As Elvis Presley said, "Values are like fingerprints. Nobody's are the same, but you leave 'em all over everything you do."

Virtual social media platforms now mimic the physical stages. With a simple scroll of the page, you can easily see the highlight reels of everyone else's life. We forget that social media is highly curated. We highlight only what we want other people to see. And even from the pieces we do see, it's impossible to know the true story behind the image. Since we don't know the real story, we create our own. And our version is usually a far cry from reality.

The key to your success is not in mimicking others.

The key to your success and to what you actually want is in becoming more of who you already are.

It's about knowing what you truly value and making decisions based on those values. Once you are clear on your own values, and affirm them to yourself and for yourself, the decisions you'll make will seem effortless. After years of trying to copy others, however, it can feel like awfully hard work to get back to yourself. And once we get there, it's a vulnerable space. *Will others like me? Will I even like myself?*

The more yourself you become, the more the right people will like you. Once you become more fully you, you'll attract the right communities and the right opportunities that are aligned with your values.

I've found becoming more "me" to be such a gratifying and life-giving experience. No competing is necessary when you're being the fully expressed version of you. Living fully in your values is living fully self-expressed and alive. And, oh, how the world needs more people who are living fully expressed, authentic lives!

DETERMINING VALUES

Have you ever scolded yourself for being lazy like I have? Perhaps you've procrastinated with a project you didn't want to do. I've struggled over the years to start the new business, to make the client calls, to write the handwritten notes, to develop the plan, to call a friend, or to schedule the appointment.

Consider for a minute that it is not laziness. Take an honest look at other areas of your life where you have been wildly productive. We all have those areas where we can do something as if time doesn't exist—instead it flies by as we complete something easily and effortlessly.

It's not laziness.

It's also not a lack of accountability.

I often have coaching clients who ask me to hold them accountable to their goals and objectives in life and business.

But...

Accountability is an inside job.

Accountability has more to do with identity than anything else. If you aren't following through with the actions that align with your goals, if you find yourself resistant to them, chances are you don't have a strong image in your mind of the *you* who naturally takes the action. Can someone really force you to do something you don't actually want to do? Do you really want to be pushed along in life? Or would you rather feel effortlessly pulled ahead?

You're not lazy. You're also not inherently an unaccountable person. *You have a lack of clarity on your personal values.*

When we find ourselves not wanting to do something we've told ourselves is important, or we are not acting in alignment with what we say we want, we're facing resistance. Get curious as to what the resistance is about. When we get curious about the resistance, we usually find that we are unknowingly violating one of our core values. Once you have an understanding of your core values, achieving your goals will be much more effortless.

My personal life core values are community, harmony, freedom, fun, and growth. And I'm excited to help you discover yours. On the following page are a list of value words to get you going. You can also find a deep dive into this topic in our community at www.TheMAGICMom.com. Start by highlighting or circling the ones that really speak to you. Look for the words that give you energy, resonate with your heart and mind, and generally give you a good gut feeling. Continue this process until you have no more than five words. Ideally, get down to your top three.

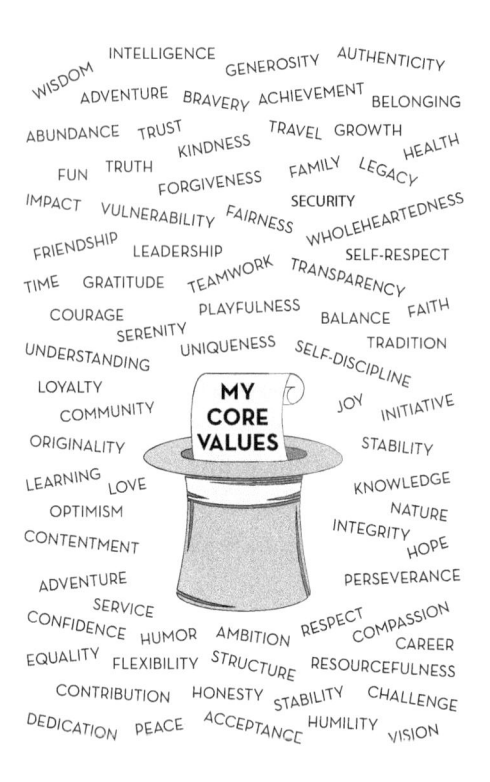

WISDOM INTELLIGENCE GENEROSITY AUTHENTICITY
ADVENTURE BRAVERY ACHIEVEMENT BELONGING
ABUNDANCE TRUST TRAVEL GROWTH
KINDNESS HEALTH
FUN TRUTH FAMILY LEGACY
FORGIVENESS
IMPACT VULNERABILITY FAIRNESS SECURITY WHOLEHEARTEDNESS
FRIENDSHIP LEADERSHIP SELF-RESPECT
TIME GRATITUDE TEAMWORK TRANSPARENCY
COURAGE PLAYFULNESS BALANCE FAITH
SERENITY
UNDERSTANDING UNIQUENESS SELF-DISCIPLINE TRADITION
LOYALTY
COMMUNITY **MY CORE VALUES** JOY INITIATIVE
ORIGINALITY STABILITY
LEARNING LOVE KNOWLEDGE
OPTIMISM NATURE
CONTENTMENT INTEGRITY HOPE
ADVENTURE PERSEVERANCE
SERVICE
CONFIDENCE HUMOR AMBITION RESPECT COMPASSION
CAREER
EQUALITY FLEXIBILITY STRUCTURE RESOURCEFULNESS
CONTRIBUTION HONESTY STABILITY CHALLENGE
DEDICATION PEACE ACCEPTANCE HUMILITY VISION

It's more than okay to take your time going through this process. For some, this process will be a quick one, but for most, like me, it will be longer and quite introspective. Print out the list and take it on a walk with you. Sit out in nature and take your time speaking the words aloud. Close your eyes and visualize the words. Which ones have the most meaning to you? Try them on. How do these words make you feel? Where do you see them show up in your life, relationships, business, and other areas?

Identity is driven from vision. It sounds easy to start with a vision, yet it's not always simple. Vision can be cultivated. Seeing something bigger for your future typically means letting go of your limitations of the past. Aligning your vision with your passion can be magical. Make time to connect to yourself and to what you really want over this next year.

In the goals section, we looked at different areas of life (spiritual, relationships, vocation, physical health, emotional health, fun, and finances). If you want to take an even deeper dive, you can determine your separate subset of values for each one of these areas individually. The first and most important set of values, however, are your overall life values, which act as umbrella over all of the other areas.

Your core values for life tend to stay fairly stable, though revisiting them regularly to do a check-in will help keep you on track to building an authentic, joy-filled life. If we are going to build your life and business starting with your core values, let's make sure we build a life you're excited to live in!

WHEN YOUR VALUES ARE CLEAR, YOUR DECISIONS ARE EASY.
Telling my girls about the opportunity to climb Kilimanjaro was an exciting yet scary one for me. They were all still so young at the time (eleven, nine, six, and three), yet I knew I wanted to seize this once in a lifetime opportunity *with* them and *for* them.

In my gut, I knew that "Yes!" was the only answer for this trip. Energetically, I was drawn to the opportunity, and logically, it made a ton of sense to support such a great cause.

I remember talking to Karissa (eleven) about the opportunity first. We were sitting in my parked car. I had my seatbelt still on and turned to her in the passenger seat. I told her how Ms. Belinda had asked me to consider this opportunity to go to Rwanda, the Democratic Republic of Congo, and finally Tanzania to climb the mountain with a summit on International Women's Day. I shared with her that the goal was to meet women, hear their stories, and raise money for programs to help these women affected by violence in war zones. She was listening so intently. I knew she was wondering how my trip would affect her. I told her I would be away for eighteen days. For an eleven-year-old little girl, it might as well have been a year. This is when the floodgate of tears opened—her first, and then me right behind her.

I remember starting to ramble a bit after that moment to try and logically explain the trip when she stopped me and said, "You said 'yes,' didn't you? You have to say yes. Those women need you to do this."

She knew that as a little girl it would cost her to have her mom be far away for what seemed like an eternity. But… our internal values were aligned, so although it was a hard decision emotionally, it was still an easy one to make.

When big or important decisions come, how do you know you're choosing wisely? There's always the coin flip, Magic 8 Ball or the good old pros and cons list.

Instead, let your values be your guide.

My number one life value is community. At the time of the Kilimanjaro trip, I craved community in a way I never had before. I was secretly desperate for deeper connection and friendships with like-minded women. I was craving new relationships outside of the business world with which I was all too familiar. I was wanting to have fun, experience growth, and do so in a way that felt authentic and true to myself. As I considered all of my core values, the trip to Africa checked every one of the boxes for me. The season of life was right, and it was in alignment with my most closely held values, personally and those of our family. Because Seth and the girls also knew my values, they gave a resounding yes to the trip, even though the sacrifice they were making was a hefty one.

Holding tightly to your values will keep you on a path toward a destination that is yours and only yours. To hold tightly to your values, first identify them. Share them with those who know and love you best. Post your values in a place you will see daily and often. Whenever you have a decision to make, reference your values as the filter and watch how easy it becomes. Decisions that used to be difficult are no longer. The peace that floods your soul knowing you made a decision congruent with your values is life giving.

The race through life is only with yourself. Your values are there to guide and affirm you along your chosen path toward a life that is of your own design and choosing. As you live a values-driven life, you'll move through your days with increased confidence, ease, and grace. You'll be modeling a process of decision-making that your daughter will be able to carry with her as she creates her own life by design.

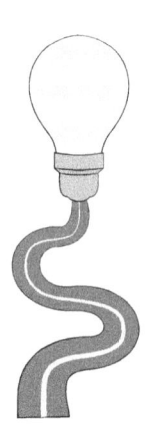

THE PATH TO MAGIC

1. Think of a high point in your life. What does it suggest about what you value?

2. Do the same exercise with a low point or a hard decision. Think of one, and consider what it reflects about your values. Were any of your values violated, and how would you know?

3. Which life decisions will be affected by knowing my core life values?

4. Who else is it important to that I share my values with so we can be on this journey together?

5. What habits can I adopt that will allow me to engage with my values on a regular basis?

CHAPTER EIGHT

Go

"I had to make you uncomfortable otherwise you never would have moved."

—LIFE

MAGIC Moms know a secret: It's okay to let your daughters go. In fact, in order to grow, they *must* go. Raising entrepreneurially spirited daughters means letting go a bit sooner than you might prefer. Your daughter isn't the only one who gets to grow in the process, Mom.

SAFETY ISN'T REAL
Safety is a myth. It's made up. Not real. And completely relative.

Getting in the car could be considered unsafe. There's the possibility of choking on a piece of steak at dinner. Does that make it unsafe to eat? Hopping a plane to a beach in Mexico has the possibility of crashing or being taken over by a cartel.

Swimming in the ocean leaves me with the chance of being eaten by a shark.

We take calculated risks every single day.

Merriam-Webster defines safety as: "freedom from harm or danger: the state of being safe."

But living life isn't safe. Not even in the slightest bit. Never has been and never will be. My safety isn't guaranteed, and neither is yours. The curve bends to zero for us all.

As moms, we tend to set ourselves up for failure by telling our daughters we are here to keep them safe. I don't see that as my work at all. My job is to coach her so that she makes the best choices possible given the situation she encounters.

If we see our work being to keep her safe, we are doomed from the start because it just is not possible. Now, I'm not talking about letting your toddler run into a busy street (please do go grab her if she does!), but I am saying that our job is to be the guide who helps her make good decisions. Not to be the hero who saves her. She needs to be her own hero in her own story.

If we do our jobs well, Mom, we won't be in the spotlight. Our daughters will. Instead, we'll get the joy and privilege of being the guide.

UNCOMFORTABLE GROWTH: SAN DIEGO EDITION

I have several stories that likely would have had one of my readers calling Child Protective Services on me for not being "safe." Again, a completely relative and arbitrary line. You'll find that one of our family values is "adventure," so travel stories abound in our household.

When Karissa was eleven and Lorra nine, we took them to a personal growth conference in San Diego. The event had five thousand attendees in the San Diego Convention Center. Our hotel was near the convention center, and when we arrived Karissa wanted to take a nap. The rest of us, however, were ready to explore. So we went for a walk in the adjacent Gaslamp district while Karissa napped. Not a big deal, except Karissa's cell phone was an old flip phone. Trying to text on it took an eternity. And when trying to make a phone call, she could hear the other party, but her microphone was broken, so we couldn't hear her.

While Karissa napped, Seth, Lorra, and I had a great time exploring some stores and outdoor farmers markets in downtown San Diego.

And then I got the text from Karissa: WHERE ARE YOU?!?!

So I called her. I knew she could hear me, but I couldn't hear her verbal replies. I gave her the exact directions on how to meet us where we were. And then we left it to her to find her way to us.

Risky? Yes, slightly. But oh so calculated. Since safety isn't a real thing, I desperately wanted to figure out how I could help her learn the skills she would need to successfully navigate life.

The adrenaline she must have felt—scared and excited all at the same time. I certainly felt it on my end too.

But I knew what a valuable lesson this was for her. I was empowering her to find her own way in a big city. She would have to be alert and aware. She would have to follow street signals and crossings. She might need to talk to a stranger to ask a question. She might get frustrated and just go back to the hotel and wait. Or she might push through and find us.

The whole thing wasn't more than fifteen minutes, though it certainly seemed longer in the moment. She texted us once to ask a question to make sure she was on the right path to finding us.

And find us she did. It sure felt like more than fifteen minutes to all of us, but it has become a fond memory and an empowering lesson for her. The confidence she had from that experience was tangible. I could see it in her face, smile, energy, and posture every time I heard her tell the story. The event took mere minutes, but the confidence she gained from it continues to grow.

As a mom, determining the lines of your comfort zone and, just outside it, your challenge zone is important to do. In order to grow, we need to leave our comfort zone and walk regularly in our challenge zone.

How do we determine when and how we'll leave the comfort zone? Our values determine those decisions. In this case, we valued empowerment and adventure. We knew that for Karissa, we would be empowering her to make choices on her own. We would be living more adventurously than usual. We also had the opportunity to affirm all of the amazing qualities she has—courage, determination, street smarts, and the willingness to try something new—that enabled her to find us.

Mom, where are you winning in this area now? And, what are other areas where you are playing it too safe with your daughter? If you take a hard look at your parenting, are there places you may want to explore opportunities to allow your daughter to grow more? What areas do you want to be able to affirm in her more, and how can you create the opportunities for this to occur more in everyday life?

UNCOMFORTABLE GROWTH: SOUTHWEST AIRLINES EDITION

Our family is grateful for Southwest Airlines allowing children to fly solo at age twelve without a chaperone. We've certainly used this as a growth opportunity in our home. When Lorra was fifteen, she wanted to fly to Grand Rapids, Michigan, for an apprenticeship opportunity with a nonprofit organization based there called One Million Thumbprints (the same organization I supported on my Kilimanjaro climb).

We dropped her off at the Baltimore airport, and my husband asked me, "Were there no direct flights to Grand Rapids available?"

"Yes, there were."

"Were they way more expensive?"

"Actually, no. The nonstop direct was actually a few dollars less."

Seth gave a puzzled look.

"I wanted her to learn to navigate an airport plane change by herself."

Lorra had been used to traveling with just her older sister, Karissa. Together, they were pros. But that largely came because Karissa was the kid you wanted to have in your group project in school. You knew she would just get it done and everyone else was along for the ride to getting an A.

I wanted to see what Lorra could do on her own.

Lorra called and texted me way more than Karissa ever did. She kept me on the phone as she read signs and had to figure out which way to get to her next gate in the Chicago Midway maze.

And then her phone was almost dead. So she had to figure out a solution.

And then her flight was delayed. So she had to navigate her options.

And when she felt comfortable again, she let me off the phone to talk to new friends she had made at the gate.

Some of you moms are probably freaking out right now. May I remind you (and I'm in this camp too) that some of us did exponentially more ridiculous and seemingly "unsafe" things ourselves at these ages—all without cell phones.

Again, the values we personally held here were empowerment, adventure, and independence. Because I hold these values as a mom, I created opportunities for the attributes to become a reality for our daughter with a calculated safety risk. Giving Lorra this opportunity bolstered her confidence to literally fly on her own.

UNCOMFORTABLE GROWTH: TONY ROBBINS EDITION
This final story I'll share here is a family favorite to date. We had just moved to Austin, and Lorra wanted to go to Miami for a Tony Robbins Unleash the Power Within (UPW) conference. She had already been once with Seth at age twelve, but she wanted to go again.

As we had just moved to Austin two months prior, we told her it wasn't something that was in our budget. We said this instead of saying "No," which is what I really wanted to say, but which isn't in line with MAGIC parenting. Instead, we adopted a mantra of, "Yes, how?"

Lorra asked, "If I can figure out a ticket, airfare, lodging, food, and ground transportation, would you let me go?"

We said, "Yes. As long as we approve of the lodging and transportation options. I mean, you are fourteen and it *is* Miami. And, no! *You cannot stay in a hostel!*"

In my head and heart, I knew it wasn't happening. The girl had four hundred dollars to her name. *At least this will be fun to watch*, I thought. My wise husband at this point booked her a Southwest flight on points, "just in case." She had enough money for the flight, so we let her know it was held for her knowing it was fully refundable.

The girl found her hustle and went to work. As humans, we are motivated by either pain or pleasure. And this girl was motivated by wanting to go to the event more than anything. It consumed her. Her drive was relentless.

She hopped on Instagram and starting messaging around looking for a ticket to the event. They run around $800, typically. She wasn't spammy or weird, just looking for someone who might want to give her a chance. She found a few people willing to sell at a discount. Eventually, several days later, she found someone who offered her a free ticket.

Well, I'll be darned, I thought. She got one. Nearly ninety Instagram messages and some relationship building and she got one. Impressive.

But she still had a long way to go. She needed to find lodging, food, and ground transportation to and from Miami from Fort Lauderdale where her flight tickets had been booked. Good luck, girl.

Lorra had done some free internship work for a Tony Robbins Coach that year. She would transcribe his coaching calls for him so he could share them with clients. She leaned into that relationship and let him know the situation. He didn't have any answers for her but certainly wished her luck.

She also reached out to an acquaintance, Nick, who she had met at a personal growth event and who she knew was going to be speaking at the event as well. She didn't want to ask him for anything, except for ideas on how she might make it happen. He didn't have any leads for her but, again, was impressed with her tenacity and drive and wished her well.

She also reached out to Jeff Hoffman, founder of Priceline. The girls had met him at a personal growth conference, and he was inspired by their drive and excitement and entrepreneurial spirit. He told them to keep in touch, and they had. She knew he was good friends with Pitbull, who often performs at UPW, so she checked in with him to see if by chance he had any wisdom. Again, no leads, but she kept at it.

Two days before the event arrived, I was certain it was over. No big deal in my mind. She had already been to the event, would go again at some point in the future, and had made it further than I thought she would.

The day before the trip was supposed to happen, she was still working on it. I would have personally given up weeks ago. But she was still at it. Sending online messages, emails, making calls.

Seth asked me twenty-four hours before she was supposed to leave, "Can I cancel her airline ticket now?"

I was totally fine with that. It was a 6:00 a.m. flight, so I would be happy to not have to take her to the airport and be done with her obsession with going to the event. I was ready for Lorra to gracefully accept defeat in this case and to applaud her creativity, determination, and drive.

I was driving home from Walmart with my younger daughters the evening before the event when I received a phone call. It was Lorra, and she was nearly hysterical on the phone.

"Mom! I need you to listen. I found a solution to everything. I can't really explain it, but I have this woman on the other line, and she wants to talk to you. She has a place for me to stay across the street from the convention center, food is provided, and so is a ride to the Fort Lauderdale airport both ways. Please. Let me put her on and just listen, okay?"

"Uh... okay. I think."

"Hi, Mrs. Dailey. My name is Maria. My company provides housing and transportation for special guests at Tony's events. I received an email about Lorra and would be happy to help. She would be in a secure condominium building that requires a wristband to enter, and she would be with me and my fourteen-year-old daughter who is attending for the first time. I've had a chance to speak with Lorra, and I'm super impressed with her and would be honored to make something work if you feel comfortable sending her."

"Uh…" silence "…okay… can I call you back in fifteen minutes when I get home?"

When I got home, I needed Lorra to fill in some blanks.

"Lorra, how did this lady get connected to you?"

"Mr. Brian sent this email and connected us."

After reading the email and realizing that the email wasn't intended for Lorra but for another member of the Tony Robbins staff, I said, "You realize that this email wasn't intended for you, right?"

"Yeah… ugh. Okay. I'll call her back and let her know that."

Lorra called Maria back and explained the situation.

Maria told me, "I know it wasn't. And that's okay. I really want to be able to help out if possible. She seems extremely eager and driven, and honestly, she'd be a great role model for my daughter who is attending for her first time."

"Uhhhhh… okay. Lorra, does she know your budget? How much does all of this cost?"

"Yes! I told her that I was doing this completely on my own, and after airfare I only had $200."

The cost of this would be $1,500 typically, which includes four nights, food, and airport transfers.

"She said she would accept my $200 as payment in full and that she would even pick me up and drop me off personally at the Fort Lauderdale Airport," which is an hour away from Miami and would have been an $80 Uber ride one way.

So, you already know how this story goes. Don't you?

We let her go. Lorra's four hundred dollars turned into an epic adventure. I made sure she shared her location and texted me frequently until the event started and she was in her seat.

She got to the condo and realizes, through conversation, that she and this "random lady," Maria, had actually met before! They met at the first UPW event Lorra had attended two years earlier—in a sea of ten thousand people, they had actually met.

Lorra had the time of her life. She made new friends, learned incredible empowering content, and gained confidence that no amount of lectures or story telling could have accomplished. Experience is the best teacher.

Growth requires getting out of your comfort zone. We were all way out of our comfort zones in these instances, and the good that came from all of it is too much to capture with a few words. We could have played it "safe" and adventureless. But who of us is guaranteed tomorrow?

We get one life to live, and we intend to live it fully.

I want to affirm these lessons for myself and for my daughters.

LIFE REWARDS ACTION

At some point, you've got to just let her go. Let her walk to the bus stop without you. Let her get on that plane without you. Take the public transportation without you. Go to the movie without you. Go on the school trip without you. Drive to school in the car without you. Go to a friend's house without you.

There isn't an age that's right for everyone. Only *you* get to decide that one, Mom, based on your intuition and spidey senses. But what I want you to remember and consider is this: Life rewards action. Life rewards movement in a direction—any direction. We need momentum and inertia to get going. And it won't always feel safe.

The growth you're looking for is on the other side of your comfort zone.

Raising a daughter with an entrepreneurial spirit means raising a daughter who knows how to take a good, calculated risk. We never said this would be easy, but that's not what you signed up for. Is it? You wouldn't be here if it was. You're my kind of people, Mom.

THE PATH TO MAGIC

1. How have my personal views on safety affected how I live my life? How has it affected how I've shown up as a mom?

2. Who are my role models for living an adventurous life?

3. Where do I have an opportunity to get out of my comfort zone that I haven't taken advantage of yet?

4. How can I affirm my daughter when she does step out of her comfort zone?

5. What opportunities can I create for my daughter to push the boundaries of her comfort zone? How could we do this together?

PART THREE:

GRACE

"To forgive is to set a prisoner free, and to discover the prisoner was you."

—CORRIE TEN BOOM

If I gave you a property worth a million dollars but the only issue was that the well on the property was completely dry, would you want to move in?

No, you say? Me neither.

When I was a little girl, my mom took me on a trip to India to visit family. I remember joyfully going out to the well to draw water with these little buckets. It was a ridiculous amount of effort to pull the ropes to draw up just one small, heavy bucket of water, but when you don't have to do it every day, it's quite novel and fun. When my cousins saw me, they were frantically concerned the power must have gone out, which would be the only sane reason to manually draw water! But it wasn't the case. This was just my idea of a good time since it was so far from my normal Baltimore suburban life.

I've never had the good fortune to live on a property with well water. In all my years of selling real estate, I've attended a fair share of well inspections, however, which can take upward of four hours. I always knew they tested water quality and potability, and in addition they provided a vital report indicating a "gallons per minute" reading, which needed a minimum to be acceptable. After a few years in the industry and not fully understanding the test, I finally decided to ask the well inspector what it all really meant. I'm not a super detailed, technical person, so I was secretly hoping his answer wouldn't be lengthy and bore me to tears.

To my surprise, he simply said, "The purpose of a well test is to determine *how quickly the well recovers.*" Well that's deep. Isn't it?

When well water gets used, the most important information we can know about the health of the well is how fast it will recover and fill back up. Quite a brilliant metaphor for all of life. When we are depleted and without hope, what is the speed at which you recover? And how can you and I do this proactively—fill that well up as expeditiously as possible?

We can fill our own well through extending grace, first, to ourselves—also known as self-compassion—and then toward others.

GRACE-FILLED LIVING

People who are more self-compassionate are more likely to accomplish their goals. If we want to raise strong daughters, grace will be essential for us and for them.

We all tend to be our own biggest bully. We don't typically need anyone else to beat us up, as we do a great job on our own. I've certainly caught myself saying things in my head to myself that if someone said to my daughter, I'd go full Mama Bear on them.

We have another path, however, and that is to extend grace. Grace is undeserved kindness. It's knowing that all of the mistakes made are simply part of a bigger purpose and no longer shameful.

Grace encompasses compassion, which includes empathy and the desire to reduce pain. Doesn't it seem that mothers were put on this very planet to reduce pain for all of humankind? When we express gentleness, kindness, and caring toward others, we are extending compassion and understanding to meet them where they are. We create an environment of psychological safety for others to feel seen, known, and heard.

When we fail and when we experience distress and anguish, self-compassion is giving to ourselves this same exact level of grace.

Grace can show up in many forms. Sometimes it appears in words and at other times in actions.

Sometimes it's about giving grace to others, and more often than not, it's about giving grace to ourselves. Rarely a day that goes by that I don't need to have grace with and for myself. I rarely have a day when I don't need to say, "I'm sorry," to someone for something that I did or for some way that I showed up.

Simply verbalizing grace shows our humanity. I've learned that apologizing to my daughters for my behavior or my actions or my attitudes is modeling a beautiful behavior. And by doing this, I'm showing them grace. I'm showing them forgiveness. I'm showing them what it's like to be real and authentic and human. I am giving them permission to do the same and extend grace toward themselves first—and then to others.

SELF-CARE
Consider that self-care *is* a form of grace.

What is self-care maintenance? Just like how your car lights up to tell you it needs gas or an oil change, we have those lights that go on in our internal dashboard. We just tend to ignore them way longer!

I know it when my hair grows just past the point where a haircut is needed and calling the stylist should be moved up on my list. I know it when the dishes and garden have gotten the best of me or my nails are in need of a manicure and pedicure. I know it when my neck and shoulders could use the chiropractor or a massage. But somehow, as moms, we tend to push the limits on these things for ourselves. Don't we? We know it's important not to let the engine in our car burn out by skipping an oil change. But why do we allow our own internal engines to burn out on a regular basis?

According to Kristen Neff, PhD, a leading expert in self-compassion, research shows that self-compassion is connected with high levels of resilience, less reactive anger, and higher quality relationship behavior.

Have you ever sat in the car for twenty minutes in front of your house before going in?

Have you taken off some time to go get a massage and a cup of coffee by yourself?

Have you ever just eaten the piece of cake and not shared with anyone?

These are all self-care. And these are a big part of grace. Just as much as apologizing for a harsh word, angry look, or unfair punishment can be.

By modeling grace to our daughters, we're giving them an incredible gift that will pay off for generations to come.

So where do we start with grace? Lucky for us, we'll have a plethora of opportunities to practice this one on a daily basis.

THE JOURNEY TO GRACE

I wonder, now that I'm well into my forties, what I was, in fact, doing for the previous decades. In so many ways, I feel as though I have just started, in the past five years or so, to actually live. I was so busy building, creating, pleasing others, participating as a human "doing," that I failed to notice what was going on around me and most importantly, inside of me.

If I were to show you an orange and ask what would come out if I were to squeeze it, you would most likely say, "Orange juice," yes?

And you would be correct.

But *why* would orange juice come out?

Simply because that's what is inside.

When life squeezes us, whatever is inside of us is what will come out.

We can't give out what we don't have inside ourselves. We are incapable of giving grace to others if we can't first extend grace or self-compassion to ourselves. Yet, how do you even get to a place of figuring out when you need grace? Sadly most of us only notice it when it's far too late. We make excuse after excuse as to why everyone else needs us first, and we prioritize others above ourselves. Well, Mama, get off the cross; we need the wood. It's time for the martyrdom to end.

There's a reason why airplane attendants make sure we know to put on our own oxygen mask first before helping the kids. Because they damn well know we won't. We'll make sure every other human being on the plane has theirs on first, along with a snack, before we ever look for our own mask.

Yet, Mom, do you realize how many more people you could actually help if you were healthy and whole yourself—as in, if you put on your oxygen mask first? Truly. Think about that for a minute.

Our tendency to put our self-care last is a way of diminishing ourself, even hiding our self. We hide behind helping others. We hide in our generosity. We hide in our servanthood. Though based on the premise of hiding in the name of good things, when we hide, we make ourselves small to the point of being invisible. And when we are invisible, we are unknown and, ultimately, unknowable.

Is this what you want for your daughter? Me neither, friend. Figuring this out for us may mean we need to model, teach, and empower our daughters to live differently than we have been up to this point.

The journey of grace and self-compassion begins with just noticing, or what is often called "mindfulness." Notice sounds, smells, taste, and—my favorite—feelings. But in all seriousness, start with the small stuff. It's all just a practice. If you're used to scarfing down your meals, or even not eating at all, start a practice of actually sitting down to drink your coffee. What does it taste and smell like? What, who, or where does it remind you of? Just notice. Be present with yourself and that coffee—even if just for two minutes. Grace starts here.

Perhaps throughout these chapters on grace, you'll uncover some critical self-talk that surfaces. Come up with an affirmation or two to turn those around. Start practicing the art of talking to yourself with purpose and intention. Maybe grab a journal and doodle a picture or a phrase that comes to mind. Growth and change all comes through reflection. Carve out little, tiny pockets of sacred space to be present with your thoughts and your feelings so you can come back to you.

Take off your shoes and go barefoot outside for even a minute. Reconnect with the earth and the outdoors. Really take a deep breath and hold it for a few seconds before you let it all out. Notice whatever is present for you without any judgment. And if and when the tears come, let them. It's all a part of the journey.

In the following pages on trauma, busyness, and empathy, I know some stuff will come up for you as you read. I'm right here with you, so would you be willing to let whatever wants to come up to surface? Jot it down in a journal as it does so it has a home in which to rest.

Let the words on the following pages and, more importantly, the ones you write in your journal give you clues on how to best refill your well. May the recovery time of the water in the well of your soul get shorter and shorter, as you increasingly extend grace to yourself first and then to those around you.

CHAPTER TEN

Trauma

"One day you will tell your story of how you've overcome what you're going through now, and it will become part of someone else's survival guide."

—BRENÉ BROWN

LOOKING INWARD

Trauma passes down from generation to generation until someone is willing to deal with it. Let's just say I was handed a boatload of traumas from who knows how many generations. The weight of it was soul crushing, though I didn't even know how to identify it until my late thirties.

Not a single human being escapes life without some form of trauma. I thought trauma was a code word for sexual assault or some sort of life-altering death or illness. It's not. Trauma shows up in so many different forms and sizes. I used to play the game of thinking my trauma wasn't really trauma because it wasn't as drastic as someone else's experience. I diminished my own experiences with comparative trauma. And that's no good. Trauma can't—and shouldn't be—compared. You are running your own race. Your race and your pace.

When I finally started to understand trauma and own that I wasn't immune to it, I wholeheartedly decided I wasn't willing to participate in the passing down of trauma any longer. Much easier said than done, but the good news is that, despite being hard, it is the doable kind of hard. I decided I wanted to be able to look my daughters in the eyes and tell them with certainty and integrity that I did everything within my ability to deal with the trauma as best I could. I wanted to be able to tell them that I utilized all of my tools and resources to heal for myself *and* for them.

I'm not responsible for what happened to me. But I am fully responsible for dealing with it.

If I had known how hard the road ahead would be for me to accomplish this, I don't know if I would have made the same decision. So I'm glad I didn't know. In order to heal from trauma, there's hard work and there's heart work. Eliminating trauma requires full engagement of both.

In terms of my own personal traumas, I've collected an arsenal full over the years, and you probably have too. I have stories I could share from interactions with my parents (we *all* have those), stories from the playground as a little girl, or as an adult experiencing the trauma of delivering our oldest at twenty-nine weeks. I'm still collecting more stories too. I'm just grateful that the years have given me the awareness and wisdom to know how to navigate the trauma far more effectively than I used to.

As a mom of daughters, it can be quite common to see our younger little girl selves in them. While we're raising our little girl, we're also doing the work of reparenting and caring for the wounds we experienced as young girls. Often times when I react in an unfavorable way to my daughter, such as through anger or harsh words, I have to look inward. What did I experience, likely as a young girl, that caused such an unwarranted reaction? If my reaction didn't match the situation, what part of my own soul can I revisit and reparent to let the little girl inside myself know she's safe? I've found reflections like these to be some of the greatest joys of being a girl mom.

Have you accounted for any trauma that you've inherited? Has anything been passed down to you of which you are unaware? What about any "new" trauma that you're accumulating yourself? Are you planning to pass it on to your daughter?

Hint: If you're not planning to deal with it, you're by default choosing to pass it to her.

We repeat what we don't repair.

HARD WORK VERSUS HEART WORK

I was falling apart on the inside long before I fell apart on the outside. When I decided to climb Kilimanjaro in 2015, I can see now, in retrospect, that my soul was crying out for help. I was already crumbling internally; I just couldn't see it at the time. I was fixated on just being "fine." Instead, it took another three years before I fell apart on the outside too. Though I spent a lot of energy and willpower to keep it all together on the outside, I finally ran out of gas. I hit a wall. I was tired. Beyond tired, really. I was exhausted, sad, and even in despair.

I loved so much about the life we built, yet big pieces of it just didn't work for me anymore. We had built a big real estate sales business and brokerage, had four great children, spoke at conferences around the country, traveled to fun places, ate out at great restaurants, and had lots of friends. Yet inside, I felt so hollow. I felt like the business ventures and the life I had consciously helped to build suddenly changed into the very noose used to hang myself.

I remember numerous days when I was so busy with clients that I would get to the evening and realize I only had five protein shakes the entire day. Not a bit of real food.

Or the day I was driving home and I ran a red light because my brain was racing so fast.

Or the busyness of running my girls to and from school, sports, art lessons, friends' houses, sleepovers, the orthodontist, camps, activities, and church, to name a few. And these were just the places we went when everyone was healthy.

Let's not even get into the adjustments that happened on "sick days."

All good things, but at what expense?

I stopped showing up at the office. I stopped doing the activities that I had always done that would help feed my family. I stepped away from friendships and activities.

So what was the trauma? There were so many layers to peel back before I finally exposed even a bit of the root. I was unhappy with my work, my marriage, where we lived, how I felt physically—and I ran from it by keeping busy.

During this season, my husband asked me if I was sick of Baltimore, my work and business, or the marriage. My answer was simply, "Yes." All of it. I was more tired and exhausted than I even knew. I hope as you're reading this, you're unable to relate. But my gut feeling is that you have your own version of the story.

I never knew a different way to do life. I measured where I was based on other people and kept striving for more. My striving was without reason, really, except that others had more, so shouldn't I want to have more too? I never thought I had a "keeping up with the Joneses" mentality, but somehow, it had been ingrained deep within me. I only knew how to live life by comparison. Not only did I not know how to create and choose a life that I designed, I didn't even know that it was an option.

We're conditioned by society to think that we'll be happy once we have the education, or the house, or the relationship, or the designer purse, or the flashy car, or the kids.

More income, more status, more travel, more stuff. More of everything.

But it's a trap and a prison. It's more for the sake of more. And it was a part of the cycle that caused me to hit a wall.

One of my ways of coping with my distress was to keep busy. Like, nonstop every-second-of-the-day busy. Not busy with meaningful and purposeful stuff, necessarily—just plain busy. I wore busy as a badge of honor. But there is no honor in being busy. And the truth was that for me, busyness was a trauma response that enabled me to not feel pain and sadness. Yep, read that last sentence again.

If you're human, you've probably experienced this too. And if it's your normal pace, know that you're definitely not alone.

Busy is a way I behaved so I didn't have to feel.

I didn't realize that what I really wanted and needed was, as my friend Ashton says, "More and more of less and less."

I knew how to work hard. I knew how to do hard work. What I really needed, however, was heart work. I unknowingly kept busy—doing *really* good things like serving clients, team members, my family—in order to not have to sit in the pain that was actually there.

I remember different counselors saying things like, "What are your tears about?" Tears are a way in which the body is telling us that all is not well. Tears? I was so freaking busy I didn't even have the time for tears. Wasn't it the counselor's job to figure out what the tears were about and just fix it for me? Or to tell me how to fix it? I went to counseling for the three-step fix-it solutions. And I was ticked off that those weren't what I got.

I remember another counselor who asked often, "What are you feeling in your body? Where?" Nothing would make me more angry than to hear her ask it. Just the fact that I was angry was an indicator that all was not well. In retrospect, it was another clue. What did the feelings in my body have to do with anything at all, and why am I paying you to ask me that question? My inside voice was really screaming, *Just help me figure out what's going on and give me the three-step program so I can go back to being busy, please! I don't have time for this nonsense!*

Hard work is what I knew how to do. But heart work was what I needed. That was a new concept for me.

The first lesson in heart work for me was this: *The human body doesn't lie.* It simply can't. That tension in your neck and shoulders? It's telling you something. That tightness in your jaw when you're in a conversation with a client or friend? It's telling you something. That twitching in your hand? Your body is talking to you—screaming for your attention.

When I'm experiencing trauma, I sleep. That's my vice. I disappear through sleep. And sleep is a good thing, right? So no one questions it. Food would be second on my list. Hand me the chocolate and all the fries, please. What do you do? Identifying where we go during pain is an important first step in noticing. No shame—just noticing. We all need comfort, and we resort to different avenues of hiding. Addictions aren't actually the problem.

Instead, we can start to see the addictions as our guide to uncovering the trauma to address.

I still have a hard time using the word "trauma" as it relates to anything that involves me because I find it hard to not compare my trauma to that of others who have suffered such difficult and indescribable things. Diminishing my own hurt and trauma is something I did because I felt like mine wasn't as big or as important as someone else's. Minimizing my own hurt and trauma, however, doesn't take anything away from the pain and trauma someone else feels and experiences. So, I don't need to "compare" trauma. Our pain is our own to feel and navigate.

The glorious part about trauma is that there *is* a path to healing. When you tell your story to others and feel heard by another, the brain actually rewires itself. Telling your story and allowing another to empathize with you *is* healing. Have you had times with a friend where you just listened and desperately wished you could do more to help? The good news is: You didn't need to do more. By listening and offering empathy, you gave the greatest gift possible. You allowed your friend's brain to rewire and heal (Angeles, 2017).

TELLING YOUR STORY

Listening is one of my superpowers. I didn't consider it a superpower until I came to understand its healing effects. I also realize that it's what I show up to do every day in my work as a coach and as a mom. I show up ready to listen to my daughters. I'm not there to fix. I'm present to listen to what is being said and to hear what is happening in the silence. Listening can be one of your superpowers as a mom too. You don't need the answers, just the ability to listen and truly hear.

Do you have an outlet where you aren't always the one listening but are also being listened to? Hopefully, there are frequent times when an effective listener will listen to you and you can say, "I felt heard by you." Who are the people in your life who make you feel heard? What are ways in which your daughter feels heard by you?

We all have stories that need to be told and stories that we need to hear from others. What story will you tell? Whose will you listen to today?

Think about stories from your childhood—stories that you vividly remember, but you're not even sure *why* you remember them so well. Those are worth exploring. It's not by accident they left an impression.

When I was about six years old, my mom and I were at the mall in the center court area where a magician was performing on a black pop-up stage. My mom and I stood on the back left side of the semicircular configuration. I loved magic tricks and was fascinated and delighted by all kinds of showmanship.

At some point in his short little performance, he asked for a volunteer. I was extremely shy, so looking back, I'm surprised I raised my hand. I was even more startled when he called on me. I walked what seemed to be a mile up to the stage. I remember seeing a few steps off to the right, but it never occurred to me to take the steps onto the stage. Instead, I hoisted myself up onto the stage using my arms and shimmying up in my corduroy pants.

I heard laughter and I couldn't figure out why. The magician did some sort of trick, which I must have assisted with in some way, although I can't for the life of me remember what kind of trick it was.

When the trick was over, the magician very kindly gave me a red balloon animal and walked me over to the stairs and led me down the three or four black steps. I now realize that people had laughed earlier because I chose to climb up and not take the stairs.

In this moment I realized I didn't take the steps up to the stage because I did not believe the steps were meant for me.

This story has played itself over time and time again in my life as a pattern. I've believed that lots of things weren't for me, but they were for other people. What kinds of things did I believe weren't for me? Shopping at name brand stores, being at the front of a line, eating at nice restaurants, being a part of the popular crowd, getting a class ring, going to a nice hair salon, staying at a fancy hotel, playing a team sport, going to prom, being physically fit, having a boyfriend, getting into a prestigious university, getting all A's in school, having a lot of friends, speaking up for myself, getting a fancy coffee at Starbucks, building a big business, having a second home at the beach…

These were all things for other people. But not for me. Just like those stairs when I was six years old.

The list really could go on for pages. I've gone through life thinking so many things just simply weren't for me. Logical? No. My reality? Absolutely. For nearly forty years of my life, I've believed the stairs, and so many other opportunities along the way, were just not meant for me.

I'm so sad for that little girl who didn't realize all the blessings that were actually available. Those nice little treats and little luxuries? They were more than okay, and they were for me.

If that one singular interaction with a magician at age six had the ability to impact all of these events in my life, to name a few, the story was worth exploring in depth. What stories are you holding on to that are waiting to be shared with a counselor, coach, or friend? The trauma you've been holding onto—the trauma your body is telling you about—could be ready for some healing.

Allowing our daughters into some of these places of our pain at the right age is an important rite of passage. They don't need to hear all of it, but we give them an incredible gift when they get to see the real human and raw side of us as women. As her mom, only you can decide when the appropriate age is to share, but sharing demonstrates confidence and vulnerability in a way I would hope she emulates someday.

Allowing our daughters to see that not one of us escapes trauma is also a gift. They have likely already experienced trauma, and by giving it a name we allow them to start talking earlier and therefore healing earlier. Healing of our trauma is a beautiful expression of grace. What a gift you will leave for future generations as you refuse to let the same trauma pass down to the next generation.

THE PATH TO MAGIC
1. Where are the spaces and who are the people I can find to begin having conversations about possible trauma I've experienced, big or small?

2. What two or three stories come to mind from my childhood that I want to explore more deeply?

3. Do I believe my listening to another is healing for them? If yes, how can I regularly exercise my listening muscle?

4. When my daughter talks with me, does she feel heard? How do I know if she does or not?

5. When my daughter shares a problem with me, how can I practice resisting the need to jump in with advice and, instead, listen and ask more questions from a place of curiosity?

CHAPTER ELEVEN

Busy

———

"As long as I kept moving, my grief streamed out behind me like a swimmer's long hair in water. I knew the weight was there but it didn't touch me. Only when I stopped did the slick, dark stuff of it come floating around my face, catching my arms and throat till I began to drown. So I just didn't stop."

—BARBARA KINGSOLVER

As a Realtor, I was working seven days a week. Nights. Weekends. Dropping my girls off at my mom's house so I could go on one more appointment or show clients a few more houses. The more skilled I became, the more I was referred to others and the busier I became. I was always anxious and my brain never stopped. More marketing ideas, nonstop phone calls, texting while driving, ordering a spicy chicken combo with a chocolate frosty and Diet Coke from the Wendy's drive through—sometimes twice in a day.

The more in-demand I became, the more speaking opportunities presented themselves. So I hopped on more planes. It was rewarding to feel significant. But I was tired, exhausted, and weary.

If I walked around with a handle of Tito's all day bragging about how much I like to drink, surely you'd get me some help. But if I brag about how busy I am, I get rewarded instead.

Busy, my friend, is an addictive substance that leads to death. No different than alcohol. No different than drugs.

In early December 2018, I walked into my office and hated the fact that I had a glass door, because the tears just wouldn't stop. I felt tired and trapped. And I didn't even know what I wanted to escape. I just knew I needed a change. I needed oxygen so I could breathe.

On the inside, I was dead. I was unrecognizable even to myself.

All I could do was cry. And this time, I couldn't make it stop.

Have you ever felt like you just needed some oxygen? Ever been in a physically wide-open space and still felt like you were suffocating?

That was me.

I kept busy so I didn't need to feel the pain. I kept busy so I didn't need to *feel*, period. I had no idea, however, that I was doing this. The behavior was unconscious wrapped in the guise of being responsible and serving others.

Numerous times I'd procrastinate on projects or tasks. I thought it was because I was lazy. I even procrastinated writing this book for years. But it wasn't because of laziness. I've always known how to work hard and have never been afraid of it.

I procrastinated because it would put me in a place where I needed to feel more negative and hard feelings—fear, insecurity, confusion, shame, hurt, frustration, boredom, and self-doubt. I wasn't avoiding things I necessarily hated. I was avoiding things of which I was afraid. And funny how the things we are most afraid of are usually the ones worth pursuing most.

BREAKING UP WITH BUSY IS A DECISION
In the words of the great philosopher, Ferris Bueller, "Life moves pretty fast. If you don't stop and look around once in a while, you could miss it." I decided I didn't want to miss any more of my own life.

Yet, what does it mean to "decide"?

According to the Online Etymology Dictionary, we see the word "decide" literally means "to kill off."

When we decide, we are cutting off other options. We are actually killing off other possibilities.

Breaking up with busy is a decision to be made. I made the decision in December 2018. The tears wouldn't stop, which was a gift my body was giving me, though I surely didn't consider it one at the time. Tears are a way the body lets the pain come out. Please, never apologize for your tears. When you have them, notice them and listen to what your body is communicating to you. But please, don't apologize. Let your daughter see that the tears aren't meant to be stuffed back down.

I immediately called one of my closest friends and simply said, "I don't know what to do." I know how to do hard things, but dealing with this level of emotion wasn't in my wheelhouse. I didn't have a how-to manual with the three-step program. I so desperately wanted one.

I was ready to walk away from my career, my marriage, and the life I had built. I was robotic in my work. My marriage was on autopilot. And I just kept busy until the wheels fell off the bus.

I was angry. I had followed the script perfectly. I had good grades in high school. I went to college and graduated with a double major. I got married. I got a great job right out of school and a master's degree. I had kids. I built a great business and a career. I had nice clothes, lots of stuff, and went on vacations.

And that's where the societal script stopped.

And so did I. That's where I broke down.

What's after school, marriage, work, and kids?

(Cue the crickets.)

When I turned that next page, it was blank. The script was a terrifying white page.

I thought I was living my own life. But I wasn't. I was living out what I thought I *should* be doing according to "the script."

I wasn't living my own life.

I had convinced myself I was living my own life, but I was living according to "the societal script." It was like playing a game of musical chairs and then the music stops. I kept spinning around realizing there was no music to keep me dancing around and no chair for me sit in.

But what am I supposed to do once the script ends? What's next? Keep doing this for the next forty years or so and then die? I came to the realization that many people do merely continue on with the robotic motion of work, caring for kids, marriage, divorce, and eventually death.

I saw other people get to the end of the "societal script" and then loop it… They'd go back to school for another degree. They'd finish raising their kids. They'd get divorced. They'd go on dates. They'd get remarried. And then? It's a blank script again. But this time, they were closer to the end of their life, so there wasn't much of a script left to write. They'd filled up their pages with "busy."

Mom, whose life are *you* living? Are you living one based on a societal script *or* one you are actively creating in real time?

For forty years I thought I was living my own life, but I wasn't. And now I had a choice to make.

I could continue to keep being "busy" by doing, doing, doing. Or, I could slow down and learn to start "being."

Surely, I dared to hope, there must be a better way.

I wanted *so* desperately to start writing my own script. To write my own "rest of the story." But I knew I had to break up with busy in order to get to this unknown place of "being."

Whose life was I living? At this point I realized I had no idea, but I knew it wasn't my own, and I knew it wasn't okay with me. Making the decision to break up with busy is the first step to finding real change.

CREATING MARGIN
Taylor Swift sings a catchy song about "Blank Space." Whenever we moms have a blank space, instead of leaving it blank, we tend to write in everyone else's name—except our own. Once we decide to break up with busy, it's time to keep the blank space blank. For most of us, it means removing things from our calendars and schedules to build in blank space and margin. Learning and growth doesn't come from the doing; rather, it comes from times of reflection. And without white space, we have no opportunity to reflect and grow.

Where do your best thoughts, ideas, and daydreams surface for you? Mine come as I'm drifting off to sleep, in the shower, while I'm driving, or while I'm getting a massage. Sometimes they come while I'm taking a walk, sitting by the pool, or weeding in the garden. The best creative ideas I've ever had can be attributed to having blank space, and usually it's while I'm participating in one of those activities. A common thread to those activities is they all allow the mind to wander. They afford an opportunity for the mind to drift and to be curious. The typical self-imposed mental boundaries are lifted, and in that freedom, creativity can be unleashed. Unstructured space is something that we desperately need more of in our lives.

Up to this point the script of my life looked like a term paper with absolutely no margins or spacing, just one giant run-on sentence in size seven font. I had tried to fit as much as humanly possible onto the page so there was no white space at all. That was my life. It was what I considered to be living—but I was wrong. Instead, it was a slow death.

During my coaching sessions, one of the biggest complaints I hear from women is: "I don't have the time!"

We don't *have* the time because we don't proactively choose to *make* the time. Creating the time by reprioritizing our activities based on our values is our responsibility. And the only way to know how to prioritize is to create the margins to think and reflect. To create the margin, we need to become more skilled at saying no to things—even things that are good.

When I finally wore myself out to the point of utter despair and exhaustion, I started down a different path thanks to counseling and coaching and finding some new life-giving models to follow.

I needed to seek out others to learn how to redraw boundaries and margins in my life. Drawing boundaries and holding them is hard, y'all. It meant people would be mad at me. I wasn't used to people being mad at me because I always found a way to keep them happy while creating an internal war within myself I didn't even realize. I sacrificed my own peace for the agenda of others. Drawing boundaries for yourself means people will be upset. It will confuse people because it's not the way things have been. When you draw new boundaries, you're doing it for you—*not* for other people. The boundaries are for your own protection.

BREAKING UP WITH BUSY REQUIRES CHANGE
The things that got you to being busy will look different as you break up. We will come to realize for every time we say yes, we are automatically saying no to something else. For example, if I say yes to meeting a work client at 6:00 p.m., I'm by default saying no to dinner with my family. If I say yes to two weeks in Mexico, I may be saying no to a business opportunity.

Breaking up with busy will mean learning how to say no in new and different ways.

Let's practice some new ways to say no—especially for those of us, me included, who have a hard time saying it! I'm the one who replies, "Maybe," even if I know I can't go to the party, just because I don't enjoy saying no.

Here are my top five favorite ways to say no. But on the next page, in honor of my age, you'll find forty-four ways to also say no. Get in front of a mirror and practice saying all of them out loud!

1. You're so kind to offer, but I can't.
2. It just won't fit right now.
3. Thanks for thinking of me, but I can't.
4. I wish I could make it work.
5. No. (It *is* a complete sentence.)

1. NO THANKS, I WON'T BE ABLE TO MAKE IT.
2. REGRETTABLY, I'M NOT ABLE TO.
3. YOU'RE SO KIND TO THINK OF ME, BUT I CAN'T.
4. SOUNDS GREAT, BUT I CAN'T COMMIT.
5. RATS! WOULD'VE LOVED TO.
6. THANKS FOR THINKING OF ME, BUT I CAN'T.
7. I'M NOT THE GIRL FOR YOU ON THIS ONE.
8. I'M LEARNING TO LIMIT MY COMMITMENTS.
9. I'M NOT TAKING ON NEW THINGS.
10. IT DOESN'T SOUND LIKE THE RIGHT FIT.
11. I'M NOT SURE I'M THE BEST FOR IT.
12. NO THANK YOU, BUT IT SOUNDS LOVELY.

NO

13. IT SOUNDS LIKE YOU'RE LOOKING FOR SOMETHING I'M NOT ABLE TO GIVE RIGHT NOW.
14. I WON'T BE ABLE TO DEDICATE THE TIME I NEED TO IT.
15. I'M HEAD-DOWN RIGHT NOW ON A PROJECT, SO WON'T BE ABLE TO.
16. I WISH THERE WERE TWO OF ME!
17. I'M HONORED, BUT CAN'T.
18. I'VE GOT TOO MUCH ON MY PLATE RIGHT NOW.
19. I'M NOT TAKING ON ANYTHING ELSE RIGHT NOW.
20. I WISH I COULD MAKE IT WORK.
21. I WISH I WERE ABLE TO.
22. IF ONLY I COULD!

23. I'D LOVE TO – BUT CAN'T.
24. DARN! NOT ABLE TO FIT IT IN.
25. NO THANKS, I HAVE ANOTHER COMMITMENT.
26. UNFORTUNATELY, IT'S NOT A GOOD TIME.
27. SADLY I HAVE SOMETHING ELSE.
28. UNFORTUNATELY NOT.
29. APOLOGIES, BUT I CAN'T MAKE IT.
30. I'M FLATTERED YOU CONSIDERED ME, BUT UNFORTUNATELY I'LL HAVE TO PASS THIS TIME.
31. THANK YOU FOR THINKING OF ME. UNFORTUNATELY IT'S JUST NOT A MATCH.
32. NO, SORRY, THAT'S NOT REALLY MY THING
33. I CAN'T MAKE IT WORK.

NO

34. IT JUST WON'T FIT RIGHT NOW.
35. I'M REALLY BUCKLING DOWN ON MY PRIORITIES RIGHT NOW, SO I CAN'T.
36. I ONLY SAY YES TO VERY SELECT OPPORTUNITIES, AND UNFORTUNATELY THIS DOESN'T MEET MY CRITERIA.
37. THE DEMANDS WOULD BE TOO MUCH FOR ME.
38. IT'S NOT FEASIBLE FOR ME TO TAKE THIS ON.
39. I WISH I HAD ALL THE TIME IN THE WORLD.
40. MY ADVISORS WON'T AGREE TO IT.
41. MY BODY SAYS YES, BUT MY HEART SAYS NO.
42. I'M NOT THE PERSON YOU'RE LOOKING FOR.
43. I DON'T HAVE AN IOTA OF BANDWIDTH LEFT IN MY BRAIN.
44. NO.

Creating margin in your life is one of the greatest gifts of grace you can give yourself and one of the greatest gifts you can model for your daughter.

Consider whether there are sufficient margins in your daughter's life currently. Just because other families have their daughter enrolled in dance, sports, music, and a foreign language on a weekly basis doesn't necessarily make it the right choice for you and your family. Teach her, through modeling and grace, that her boundaries are important, valid, and healthy.

Plus, if you model healthy boundaries for your daughter now, she won't need to practice these same lines in the mirror as an adult!

As the world continues to speed up, the need for reflection time will be even more important. If we don't draw our own boundaries, someone else surely will. And I promise you won't like the boundaries they would want to impose on you.

FACING EMOTIONS

It's so much easier to stay busy than to face our emotions—especially the negative ones. Staying busy is just a way of numbing out so we can't feel. Once I created margin in my life, I had the time and ability to feel, and I was ready to allow myself to sit in the feelings. This was hard work. One of the truths I came to realize as I started peeling off layers of my emotions was that I didn't actually have the words or vocabulary to express my emotions. For someone with a Master's Degree in Organizational Leadership and two undergraduate degrees, the emotions I could name were four: happy, sad, mad, and scared. That was about it, and quite frankly, I was surprised and embarrassed.

Upon reflecting on my own childhood, emotions in my home growing up weren't shown often, except for anger and disapproval. I didn't have models to demonstrate healthy ways to regulate my emotions.

Grace toward myself looked like embracing new vocabulary for my emotions—naming my feelings with words I knew but didn't know how to retrieve easily. I literally carried a list of words around with me so I could pull it out anytime to find one that reflected my current emotional state. This became a practice that allowed me to have grace with myself. And when I have grace with myself, I am far more likely and capable of extending grace to everyone around me, my daughters included.

As you think about your own emotions, how many can you name? What if we were to empower our daughters to name and identify twice as many as we can? What about three times as many? How much more equipped would they be to face the world head on? I've included a list of emotion words on the following page so as you break up with busy, should you decide to do so, you can start naming your emotions as you create margin in your life.

> POSITIVE STUNNED REASSURED
> HAPPY OBSESSED TENDER
> SECURE OPTIMISTIC ACCEPTED
> CHEERFUL ELATED COMPOSED
> ENCOURAGED OVERJOYED
> MOTIVATED GRATEFUL THRILLED
> AGREEABLE EXUBERANT JOYFUL
> SATISFIED RELIEVED
> AFFECTIONATE ENLIGHTENED
> RELAXED CALM PROTECTED
> REFRESHED DARING GLAD

> DISORIENTED IRRITATED FURIOUS
> DESPERATE GROUCHY PANICKY
> BAFFLED DISTRESSED RESTLESS
> GRIEVED MYSTIFIED PARALYZED
> CONFUSED HEAVY BURDENED
> APPREHENSIVE DUPED
> INVISIBLE INJURED GUARDED
> UNLOVED IRRITATED LISTLESS
> DESERTED TENSE DISHEARTENED
> FURIOUS WEEPY FORGOTTEN
> DISCONNECTED EDGY EXPOSED

As a little girl around age seven, I was on an airplane with my mom. I remember being offended that the flight attendant actually told people, "In case of an emergency, put your own oxygen mask on first before assisting others," and I knew that meant *me*. How in the world… and *why* would this woman suggest my mother help herself before me? The flight attendant clearly didn't understand that my mother's world revolved around me and that she should—and would—help me first before herself.

Today, the roles are different. I'm the mother, as are you. And we have a choice to make every single day. When the flight of everyday life gets turbulent and those oxygen masks drop, who will get the mask first? It's been proven that by the mom putting on her mask first, the chances of both mom and child surviving are highest. By choosing to help her first, both lives are at risk. By putting your mask on first, you allow for the possibility of not only survival, but a thriving life and future.

So who will get the mask first? It's your choice, Mom.

THE PATH TO MAGIC
1. What positive function does "busy" play in my life currently? How might I be using "busy" as a coping strategy? What might I be avoiding by "behaving busy"?

2. What could be possible, for me personally, if I created more margin in my life?

3. How would increasing margin in my life affect those nearest to me?

4. Do I believe it is important to be aware of my emotions? If so, how can I increase my awareness of my own emotions?

5. What "breaking-up-with-busy" habit can I create, and who will I ask to support me in this endeavor?

CHAPTER TWELVE

Empathy

"Leadership is about empathy. It is about having the ability to relate to and connect with people for the purpose of inspiring and empowering their lives."

—OPRAH WINFREY

When Brielle was three, I heard her run into the kitchen from the family room where she was watching a *Peppa Pig* cartoon and ask her sister, "Karissa, do you know what empathy is?"

My eyes immediately darted up, and my heart skipped a beat as I knew the words that came out of Karissa's mouth next would be incredibly important. I knew Karissa understood what the word empathy was at age twelve, but how would she answer to this little one who had so much enthusiasm and wonder in her eyes?

Karissa said, "No, Brielle. I don't know. What is empathy?"

My mama heart was *so proud* in that moment. She had the emotional intelligence to know that Brielle was desperately wanting to share what it meant. Karissa knew it was a learning opportunity for Brielle and played right along beautifully so as to give her little sister the gift of sharing and connecting in that moment.

Brielle went on to say, "Empathy is when you can feel someone else's feelings."

My heart melted right there all over my sunroom floor. I'm not sure how old I was when I learned about empathy, but I'm certain it was at least two decades later or more. Thank you, *Peppa Pig*, for teaching such a valuable lesson.

Compassion, sympathy, and empathy all have similar characteristics and are sometimes used interchangeably, when there is in fact a distinction between them all. I'm most familiar personally with compassion and sympathy, as I think most of us are. Sympathy means you can intellectually understand what the person is feeling. Compassion is the desire to relieve the suffering of another. There is distance with compassion and sympathy that keeps us safe and disconnected. Sympathy is looking down at someone in a deep hole and saying, "I'm sorry you're down there."

Empathy, however, fosters connection. It requires we be fully present.

> ***Empathy is going down into the hole with another and being with them.***

It requires connecting with something within ourselves that knows the same feelings of another person. If my friend is grieving, I also have to go to a place of grieving within myself in order to have true empathy. It's a deeply vulnerable choice to have empathy for someone. Compassion and sympathy are certainly the easier of choices.

THE SUMMIT

I was on the receiving end of empathy in the most intense and personal way during summit morning on Kilimanjaro.

The morning brought with it so many mixed emotions. I had been climbing all night listening to the iPod Jessica had sent with me. I had no sense of time at all and no awareness of how long we had been climbing. I remember at some point my guide, Frank, said, "Look! Over there." As I turned around, I saw the sun rising behind me. I realized then we must have been climbing for at least six hours, probably more.

A relief comes with seeing daylight, as everything just seems ten times worse in the dark. The only problem was this—I was supposed to be at the summit by sunrise with my team. And now that I could see up in front of me because of the daylight, I saw that I was still hours from the top. I was exhausted and felt so incredibly alone. I wanted to cry but didn't even have the energy for it.

Before I had left on the trip, I visualized the climb in my mind. I visualized celebrating the summit and taking a picture at the top with all of my fourteen new friends. The thought of taking that picture and hanging it in my home was what originally kept me going. Capturing the picture symbolized my motivation to get to the top.

I knew I had to get my mind right, so I focused on what I wanted. I wanted to get to the summit to take that picture, so I kept climbing. And it couldn't have been but a few minutes later that my heart dropped. I started to see one of my teammates climbing back down toward me. Everyone else had made it to the summit and taken their pictures and were heading back down. One by one I passed my teammates as they went down as I continued up.

I was disheartened. The anguish I felt in that moment is indescribable. I wanted that picture so desperately, and in an instant the thought of having it vanished. I started talking to myself out loud to regroup and regain my focus and determination. I needed a new sense of purpose and vision to finish now. I wasn't going home to tell my girls that I quit. I wasn't going home to tell them I didn't make it to the top. As my team mates started to pass me, I started thinking about new strategies to get to the top. I started to wonder if having a different guide to help lead me would make a difference. I knew it probably would help, and it certainly couldn't hurt at this point.

I started looking for my friend Belinda to come down the mountain. I knew her guide, Ricardo, and I thought, *If she would be willing to trade guides with me, I think Ricardo could get me up the mountain.* His English was great, and he was an encouraging personality, and I knew I'd make it to the top with this change. Just the thought of this plan gave me a burst of hope and energy.

When I saw Belinda, my heart leapt. She was equally as excited to see me as she had wondered for hours where and how I was. I said, "Hey, B. I'm still going to the top. But if I can switch guides with you, I think it will be a lot easier. Would you mind if we switched?"

With more joy and enthusiasm than you can imagine and without skipping a beat, she smiled at Ricardo and said, "Hey, Ricardo! We're going back up again!"

Wait. What? I thought. "Belinda, just switch guides with me, and I'll get to the top and come back down and meet you later."

She said, "No! We're all going up together."

I cried. I ugly cried on the side of the highest mountain in Africa. I felt so seen and known in that moment by my friend, my sister. I know nothing I could have said or done would have convinced her to let me go without her. She felt my loneliness. She felt my longing and desire to make it to the top. She felt my exhaustion. And she connected with me in all of it. It would have been so much easier for her to switch guides with me and to go back down. There would have been no shame or judgment in the slightest with that.

But the vulnerability that she risked to be with me in my dark places, and her willingness to literally walk the journey with me, connected us in an indescribable way.

Belinda walked with me, encouraged me, shared her oxygen tank with me, cried with me, laughed with me, prayed with me, and went with me to the top of Kilimanjaro. The only pictures you'll see of me at the top aren't with all of my fourteen friends as I had hoped and imagined it would be, and I grieved that I wasn't able to get that picture. But what I know now is that what transpired was so much greater than anything I could have planned or imagined. Belinda was empathy personified to me that day. She demonstrated to me what I hope and desire to be to the most important people in my life, especially to my daughters.

SPECIAL TIME
Empathy is all about feeling the feelings of our daughters; being "with" them in those feelings by taking ourselves to a place where we can feel the same emotions. Connecting with our daughters in this space is a powerful way to deepen our relationship.

As we choose vulnerability in order to enter into the feelings our daughters are experiencing, it forces us to go into places in our own childhood to recall similar moments. If we allow them to, these can be moments of reflection and of healing for the little girl inside ourselves.

Several years ago, I implemented an idea, which came from a parenting class I happened upon. The concept was called "special time." As the name implies, it's time with me and my daughter alone, for whatever amount of time I designate. During this time, she gets to pick what we do. Assuming that her choice is reasonable, accessible, and within the budget and timeframe, we do it. I am consistently shocked at the things they pick. Most of the time they just want to *be* together, engaged in an activity together like a baking project or playing a card game. I've found that it's not the amount of time that matters but the quality of the time. During this time, she knows that I am 100 percent fully focused on her and our time together.

But how do you measure the quality of the time?

Try measuring by observing who is doing the most talking. Whoever does the most talking feels like the conversation went best. So make sure she's doing the bulk of the talking. You can do this by being curious. Genuine curiosity leads to asking powerful questions, which we'll talk more about in the next section.

Get out of judgment and stay in curiosity.

If we're being real, judgment is kind of fun. We're good at it as moms who have lived many more decades than our daughters. We tend to believe we have the answers to everything they are dealing with. But what if we suspend our judgment and just stay with our daughters in what they are experiencing as if we are also experiencing it for the first time too? The seemingly little things they come to us with are big things to them. So if they are big to them, it's good for us to see them in the same perspective as they do. The older we get, the bigger our perspective and the less likely little things will rock us. But when you're under eighteen, the little things *are* massive. Instead of telling her, "It's not a big deal," or "something better will come around," to sugar coat what she's experiencing, sit in the sadness and pain with her.

Sitting with someone in their pain doesn't mean you have to agree with it. It just means you're empathizing and therefore connecting and caring for your girl.

Empathy is about listening and allowing the speaker to get out everything inside of them. By hearing our daughters talk, we are actually holding space to allow their brain and neural pathways to problem-solve and heal in a productive and healthy way. So when bedtime rolls around next and she wants you to put her to bed, remember the gift you can give that she doesn't even know to ask for. Listen to her late-night ramblings with empathy. No need to give her answers or solve her problems. Just let her talk. You listen actively. It's the greatest gift you can ever give.

THE PATH TO MAGIC
1. What can I incorporate into my life each day that would increase the likelihood of responding empathetically?

2. Recall a time when you were on the receiving end of an empathetic listener. What did it feel like?

3. Who are my models for empathy that I seek to learn and grow from?

4. How would my relationship with my daughter differ if I approached each encounter with empathy?

5. Who talks more in our relationship—me or my daughter? Would a shift in that dynamic be beneficial?

PART FOUR:

INQUIRE

"We awaken by asking the right questions."
—SUZY KASSEM

"I don't know." How many times have you asked a question and heard this from your daughter?

Next time she says it, come from a place of curiosity and ask this in response: "If you did know, what would it be?"

It's like a party trick. I promise you'll be surprised at what happens next. This works on adults, too, by the way.

By asking this question, the mind opens up to possibility, whereas without the question, we remain stuck. Questions are the pathway to possibility. Questions have the ability, when thoughtfully crafted, to positively change the future before the answers ever arrive.

CURIOSITY AND CREATIVITY

The skill of inquiry—or asking great questions—is closely tied to curiosity and creativity. The more curious and creative we are, the more likely we are to believe we have many ways to solve or approach an issue and therefore ask more questions. Even as I'm writing this book, I find that I didn't write it because I had all the answers. Instead, I did it because I have an insatiable curiosity around helping moms raise brilliant, entrepreneurial-spirited daughters. As I follow the curiosity by asking questions, it leads me to great answers and even higher-level questions.

In 1968, George Land did a research study on creativity. He used it for NASA to help hire engineers and scientists and, because of its success, went on to use it for children. He tested the children at various increments and found that five-year-olds scored a 98 percent creativity rating, ten-year-olds dropped to 30 percent, and fifteen-year-olds to 12 percent. And adults? A whopping two percent. George Land's conclusion was that "noncreative behavior is learned" (Land & Jarman, 1993).

So if we've learned noncreative behaviors and been taught to accept this as opposed to asking questions, how do we use and develop this skill of inquiry?

The answer is simply practice. Developing the skill of asking great questions is an underdeveloped muscle we all have.

When I started training to become a coach, part of my homework was to write fifty new coaching questions per week. When I started, like most things, it felt like writing with my nondominant hand: awkward, clunky, and weird. Over time, however, as I started using the questions in real life, I found which ones provoked answers and which ones fell flat. This provided me feedback as to how to craft the best questions possible. I quickly found that questions starting with the words "who," "how," and "what," opened up the listener far more than a "why" question.

BECOMING CREATIVE

In 1956, Louis Mobley was tasked with opening the IBM Executive School to turn their people into creative geniuses. "Hey! Let's take a group of research and data-loving nerds and make them creative!" This was no small task. Mobley was up for the challenge, though, and had some amazing insights that became founding pillars of the school.

Mobley's Executive School was a twelve-week experiential boot camp. Instead of learning through traditional methods of lectures, the students played games and engaged in challenges and simulations. Mobley created experiments where the obvious answer was never enough.

One of Mobley's six insights was this: We don't *learn* to be creative. We must *become* creative people. In the same way, we can't pick up a book and just cognitively learn to ask great questions or be curious.

We must become curious people, and in doing so, we'll ask more inquisitive questions.

We need to start believing the obvious answers are not the answers at all (Turak, 2011).

Curiosity is the desire to learn and understand new things. If we think of the brain as a muscle that needs to be exercised and worked out, curiosity is the way in which it happens. Curiosity requires our brains to be active as opposed to passive. It requires our brain to stretch and see things in new ways.

If you were to walk into a room full of four- and five-year-olds and ask, "Who here is a great artist?" just about every hand would go up. If you do that in a workplace full of adults, or even a middle or high school classroom, the numbers would look much different, as I'm sure you can imagine. How would you answer that question for yourself? Are *you* a great artist?

What happened between age four and middle school—or even earlier? When did we stop believing we are creative? When did we begin to snuff out the thirst for curiosity?

In her book, *Courage to Grow*, Laura Sandefer opens with a story about how she was frustrated in her attempt to draw a picture of a chair. Her husband, Jeff, told her to flip the image upside down and then attempt to draw it. Because Laura was curious, unafraid of failure, and desiring to learn, she did just that. She found that by flipping the image, the left-brain quiets and the right brain goes to work instead. By using this simple technique, drawing the chair became easy.

As we get older, we need to seek out new ways to reawaken our creative spirit. It's still within you. I promise. But it won't come to the surface without some encouragement and intention.

THE POWER OF QUESTIONS
By asking powerful questions, you can change the future before the answer ever shows up. Crafting questions with positive intent and carefully chosen words allows the brain to expand and grow.

In his 1936 classic book, *How to Win Friends and Influence People*, Dale Carnegie said, "Be a good listener… Ask questions the other person will enjoy answering." In order to guide our daughters, we need to listen well. And, after listening, we can craft questions that will open her up to share. Have you ever been on a job interview, doctor's appointment, or coffee date where you wished the other party had asked you more questions? Sometimes we hold back from asking because we think we already know the answers, don't know what to ask, are unsure of what to ask, or really don't understand the power and benefits from asking questions. Asking great questions is the hallmark of every great coach. By asking great questions, we allow our daughter to become the author of solutions and ideas. And when we author something, we own it. Authorship is ownership. And when we own it, we are empowered.

Another benefit of asking questions is the interpersonal bonding that occurs when we do so. When we ask questions, we connect to the experiences, stories, and emotions of the other person. This naturally brings us closer together and, I believe, makes us more likable. Our daughters want to be known, seen, and heard. Don't we all want this, by the way? By asking her questions and allowing her a psychologically safe space to express herself, we help her to feel known.

In the following sections, we'll explore the power of inquiry when it comes to educational choices, building family traditions, and charting the course for your own life and dreams. The key to living the life you desperately want lies in all the questions you have yet to create and ask. The power is all yours when it comes to designing your daughter's future and your own. You are merely a few questions away from the life you desire.

CHAPTER FOURTEEN

Education

"I have never let my schooling interfere with my education."
—MARK TWAIN

Going to school makes me no more educated than going to Burger King makes me a flame broiled cheeseburger. Going to school makes you... a person who goes to school. No one can force anyone to learn anything.

Educating our girls is one of the most important and daunting tasks as a mom. We are tasked with making sure our daughters are well-equipped for the journey ahead. And that responsibility lies primarily in our hands. No pressure at all, right?

Ask any mom looking for a newborn daycare spot. I remember walking into the daycare center soon after I found out we were expecting our third child. Our first two daughters were already enrolled there. I knew how difficult it was to get a spot for a newborn, as there were only six coveted spaces.

When I told the daycare director I was expecting, she said, "I'm usually the second person to know aside from mom that there's a baby on the way! Moms often come and tell me even before Dad finds out!" That's how competitive and crazy finding good childcare can be.

The pressure to find a school for our children is exacerbated by the inconsistent quality of public education. The traditional school system was originally set up to educate the masses for factory jobs. The current school setup is to encourage students to be quiet, listen to the teacher at the front of the room as an all-knowing source, memorize some items to regurgitate on a test, and then move on to the next level. Rinse and repeat until we're dubbed "adults" and thrown into the world.

I recall "studying for the test" in many of my classes. The minute the test was done, the information promptly left in my brain. What I learned was to be a good test taker. I'm proud to say that I was a solid B+/A- test taker. What saddens me today as an adult is the years that were wasted because I wasn't learning to love learning.

The current educational system is archaic, rigid, and an unlikely setting to proactively nurture and foster the entrepreneurial spirit. Couple this with the astronomical cost of higher education, and it's easy to see the model is broken and screaming for change.

The current model of school as we know it might provide certain types of educational experiences, but it is severely limited. As moms, however, we cannot abdicate responsibility for true education and learning to the schools. We are responsible to find ways to supplement our daughters' education outside of the traditional norms.

Fortunately, education and school are not synonymous. School is only an optional part of education. Once you get clear on this distinction, the whole world opens up in possibility.

OPTIONS

Among the many options for education are public, private, homeschooling, and a plethora of up-and-coming alternative schooling options. The 2020 COVID-19 era shed light on the fact that our current education system has some major flaws. Overnight, the entire educational system was forced to fit into a pitiful virtual framework. Education became reduced to checking off boxes of completion. SAT and ACT tests were sidelined, becoming unnecessary overnight. Just get through it and move on to the next year. Is this *really* about learning? The COVID-19 pandemic catapulted parents into looking for new ways to educate their children.

We have always had choices in education, but never so many, and such fast-changing ones, as there are today.

Let me give you some background: I am the product of private education. My parents sent me to a prestigious private school in Baltimore. If you've ever been to town, you'll know that when people ask where you went to school, they definitely don't mean college. Baltimore is a town that prides itself in its high schools. Whenever I'm in Baltimore and asked about where I went to school, I know they don't care about my multiple undergraduate degrees or my Master's Degree in Organizational Leadership. Instead, they just want to know where I went to high school. So accordingly, I always respond with "McDonogh," and I'll immediately get nostalgic, anecdotal stories.

I was privileged to attend McDonogh for twelve years, and as I began to navigate the schooling waters for our daughters, I was curious as to the process my mom went about to choose the school for me. When I asked my mom why she picked McDonogh over the multitude of options available, I expected to hear something about how amazing the curriculum was, the fine pedigree of teachers, or all of their extracurricular activities available, but instead, she simply stated: "Well, that's easy! They provided lunch every day, and the school bus picked you up right in front of our house!" Spoken like a true tired, working, practical, single mom.

I used to be bothered by that answer, but today as a mom, *I so get it*. Never needing to pack a school lunch box and transportation taken care of both ways every day? Sold.

My husband, on the other hand, grew up in Bozeman, Montana. His high school graduating class was four hundred or so—four-times the size of mine. The size of his high school, over two thousand, was more than double the number of students at my entire K–12. He was active in debate, band, and a bunch of AP classes. In fact, when he got to college, he arrived with enough credits to be a sophomore just by virtue of the AP classes he took in high school. I'd argue that the quality of education he received was comparable to mine, just way cheaper. As the oldest of six, public school was the way to go for his family although he had been homeschooled for a year and in a private Christian school for one year.

When it came to educating our kids, and knowing that we wanted to have four, we just assumed public education. After we finished making all the daycare payments for our oldest, we felt like we were getting a raise when she entered kindergarten at our local public school. I remember being called into the principal's office before we enrolled her. Technically, Karissa missed the cutoff date by three days. She was able to test into kindergarten, and the principal wanted me to understand that by allowing her to enter kindergarten early, that would also mean she would leave home early at the age of seventeen. I'd love to say I was super concerned about it at that moment—concerned that my firstborn would fly the coop a year sooner than others her age—but the realities of the financial pressure made it so that I was glad to have her go into public school "early." The thought of the daycare payments each month and how many mortgage payments they were equivalent to was unsettling.

Luckily, we only ever had two kids in daycare at a time. I'm not sure my brain would've been able to handle three at once. We had our well-laid-out plans of daycare followed by public school and grand thoughts of investing the money we would've spent in daycare into other things like residential investment properties.

When our second daughter went to kindergarten, however, something in my mama gut just didn't feel right now that I had raised one daughter through this age. I didn't feel like she was grasping reading and writing concepts well, and there seemed to be a disconnect with what and how she was learning. When I approached teachers, they kept saying she was right on track and there was no need for concern. When she got to first grade, I remember her class having twenty-six kids. When I went in to volunteer and observe, I saw Lorra sitting at her desk, which was grouped with five boys and her. The teacher sent me a note to let me know that "Lorra is very distracted. She must have ADHD." Honestly, I wanted to ring the teacher's neck. If you put me at a table with five boys, would I appear to be attention deficit and hyperactive? Yes. Yes, I would.

I called a child psychologist friend, and we had Lorra tested for some different things. They found some dyslexic tendencies and wanted to medicate her for hyperactivity, so I did what I thought a good mom would do. I filled the prescription and started her down that road. I remember when the labels started: Dyslexic. Attention deficit. Hyperactive. And I realized how much I hated them all. I was watching Lorra turn into a dyslexic, hyperactive, attention deficit child before my eyes, and it was worse than before she was ever diagnosed. Is this who she really is? Or was I creating this with my words?

I remember when Lorra said to me, "Does taking this medicine make me smart?"

And that's when I broke.

Absolutely not. She was creative and whole just the way she was. We decided right then we were going to stop medicating. We were not going to let this crush her creative spirit or have her believe her performance was tied to a pill. We didn't know where things were all headed if we kept on the medication train, but we trusted our gut and intuition. We started asking more questions about how the medications worked and what the side effects might be. As I began to challenge the status quo, only then did I start to believe that, as her mom, I just might know more about what Lorra needed than any other "professional" did.

So, we put the medicine away, and the next school year we decided to look at a different option. We heard about a classical Christian school not too far from us, and upon investigation, her second-grade class would only be about twelve children, so we enrolled her. I never told them about the diagnoses we had received. And I waited.

When the parent teacher conference came around a few months into the school year, I asked how she was doing. They raved about her work and her creativity and what a great addition she was to the community. Not a single mention of the issues that were brought up only a few months prior.

In her next few years, the issues of ADHD and dyslexia never resurfaced. She flourished in just about anything that required creative thought. When the musical *Hamilton* came out, her love for words and poetry emerged. She even wrote a personal note to Lin-Manuel Miranda expressing how much she loved his musical, and to her surprise, he replied with a handwritten note!

Lorra was thriving in her new environment. She went from troublemaker and distraction to creative genius. It just depended on which environment she was in and which leadership she was under. We had smooth sailing until we hit another storm in seventh grade. We had hoped we had found the solution for the long haul, but alas, seasons change. And one size doesn't fit all. Lorra's creative spirit started to hit the boundaries of her school as she began to feel trapped by the academic structure. Lorra was being asked to conform to a system that she just didn't fit within. We knew she was a smart, creative kid, but in the confines of tests, she sure wasn't measuring up by the numbers. I began to feel some similar gut feelings as if she was in second grade all over again.

Meanwhile, our oldest daughter was a freshman at a different private high school. Karissa chose this high school because of a prestigious Women in Medicine program they offered. She was in a season in life where she believed she wanted to be a doctor, so it seemed like a natural fit. She was awarded an academic scholarship to attend and was admitted into a wonderful program.

My mother-in-law, Carol, has always quoted Mark Twain for as long as I've known her: "Never let your schooling interfere with your education." It never truly clicked for me until we had our own daughters. Seth and I determined we would send our kids to public school as long as it worked for our family. For some families, it works for the entire course. For others, it doesn't—and we're left to make choices. We didn't really know what that meant at the time we crafted this philosophy but trusted we would recognize it when it showed up. And boy, did we ever! I remember the precise day when we realized our girls' schooling *was* interfering with their education.

I remember the day Karissa came home and said she had been called into the principal's office. The principal's office? Uncommon words in our home. This was a kid who did no wrong. She was kind, introverted, good natured, and a great student.

She was called to the principal for missing too much school.

Perhaps I looked up too long and missed an area where Karissa wasn't doing well in school, so I inquired. Nope. That wasn't it. Her grades were all A's and B's.

My next question to Karissa was, "What exactly did they teach last week that was more important than you attending a Tony Robbins event where you walked on fire?"

I found it providential that these events with both girls occurred in close proximity. Both schools expressed that school rules were being violated. Karissa was missing too much school, and Lorra wasn't measuring up on testing. Yet, our family felt violated in the way we wanted to educate our girls.

I was internally ecstatic about recognizing what was happening. *This is exactly what Mark Twain was talking about!*

But now what?

I had no idea what other options existed. And the thought of starting over to find a new solution was daunting. Not to mention thinking of having four girls in three different locations or more. And I was tired. My career didn't leave much room for projects such as "find another schooling option for at least two—if not all four—of our daughters."

I started to just "fit in" as much research on new options in any way I could. I asked questions of everyone, everywhere. I listened to podcasts. I started to get curious about learning—and about teaching kids *how* to learn instead of focusing in on test scores alone. I tapped social media, moms' groups, friends in the education sector, homeschooling groups—nothing was clicking.

About a month later, Seth attended a retreat with the Front Row Dads, a group of men who are dads first and business owners second. He came home, handed me a book he received from one of the speakers at the event, and said, "You should start a school." I laughed and put in on my nightstand for months.

Well, you can probably guess what happened next. I don't usually cry when reading books, but cue the waterworks. I devoured the book *Courage to Grow*, by Laura Sandefer. I felt like she had absolutely *nailed* what I believed about how school *could* be. I was so moved by how she and her husband Jeff thought about education and how bravely they navigated the journey with their own children. I knew I wanted everything in that book, but there was no Acton Academy in our immediate area.

And, as if I needed more confirmation we were on the right track for our girls, Karissa and Lorra both read the book, unbeknownst to me. Karissa, who was fourteen years old at the time, read it first and was captivated. Lorra, who was twelve and didn't even love to read at the time, read it cover to cover and burst into our bedroom unannounced. "I finished this book, and I'm going to Acton. I know there are locations in Washington DC, Michigan, and Texas. Who do we know that I could go live with so I can attend?"

Whoa. They felt it too.

My brain started to get some crazy thoughts. The newfound energy that came with all of this new knowledge was invigorating. I had no idea how any of this would work, but I knew it just had to somehow.

We began to question everything. We looked at our family values, the life we had, and the life we wanted. We questioned what was right for each daughter individually. There isn't always a one size fits all solution for kids, as much as it would be convenient for our schedules. As busy as life is these days, do we prioritize our work schedules? The kids' schedules and activities? Their interests and curiosities? My own sanity? I'm pretty sure you can relate.

We questioned what a new educational model like Acton would offer. We found Socratic learning, learning to learn, autonomy, apprenticeships, business fairs, critical thinking, self-paced learning, the understanding that every hero (or student) is on their own hero's journey—among so many other things. It turned schooling as I had always known it on its head.

We found that it fit beautifully with how we wanted to educate our girls. We also believed wholeheartedly they would be able to thrive in this new environment instead of being told to sit quietly for hours on end and regurgitate answers for the sake of the test.

As we questioned our own desires, we became certain we were more interested in the girls loving to learn and following their interest and passions than we were about any test score. We asked ourselves: Wouldn't it be cool for the girls to discover their calling in the world *before* they graduated from high school instead of searching for the next twenty-plus years?

The Acton model also would allow us to travel freely through the year. Conferences and personal growth opportunities were not only allowed but encouraged. Some of the events we've taken the girls to? Landmark, Tony Robbins, Brian Buffini's Mastermind Summit, One Life Fully Lived, Gary Keller's Quantum Leap for Kids, Neurolinguistic Programming trainings, XChange, and Fambundance to name a few—some perhaps you've heard of, and others a bit more obscure.

We always look for opportunities for our girls where they can be the youngest in the room and learn even one thing. Many of these events have opportunities for "child care" where you can pay for group babysitting or field trips while, as the parent, you attend the conference. Several times we realized, if we're going to be paying for the conference or for a sitter, we'd rather they be in the conference learning *with* us instead! Even if they were to play on an iPad during the event, they would still be learning and growing, and that was invaluable in our eyes.

Acton seemed like a resounding "Yes!" from all six of us, which truly was a miracle in itself. But now what?

CHOOSE YOUR PATH
Asking great questions can lead to answers you may or may not be ready for. It can feel like opening Pandora's box as you go into the unknown.

By following my curiosity around learning and education, we started to hit some walls around the practical steps of achieving our objectives. I pursued the path of school ownership and was awarded franchise rights to open an Acton of our own. But it didn't solve our immediate issues, as our school couldn't open on day one as a K–12, so our older girls were still without a solution, and I was frustrated. I felt so close to a solution yet a million miles away simultaneously.

In January 2019, we were attending a personal growth conference in Breckenridge, Colorado, along with several other families. As we sat in a session about family values and goal setting, our friends, Mike and Lindsay from Pennsylvania, graciously shared their personal family goals. Immediately when they put them up on the board, my eye zeroed in on the bottom right side, which said: "Move to Austin this fall and enroll kids in Acton."

I nudged my husband. I said, "I don't get jealous much, but whoa. I want *that*." I could have wallowed in the jealousy, but instead, I allowed it to become a breadcrumb. I asked myself, "What if I allow the things that spark jealousy to be a guide to revealing the very things my heart actually wants?"

Austin is where the original Acton Academy was founded. I had always wanted to live in a warm climate and have always loved the South. I had desperately been wanting to move for years, but never knew where. Keller Williams International, the company of which we already owned a franchise, was also based in Austin. We had several friends who had recently moved their families there as well.

And just like that, the conversation started—one of questions and very few answers…

- Could we run our business remotely to be able to move?
- Was moving in the best interest of our family?
- What could this adventure look like?
- How could this next season of life be more than we could ask for or imagine?

Asking great questions can bring chaos, so be ready to entertain and welcome it should you find yourself in the same position I was in. While we were asking these magical questions, I was simultaneously living out the pieces we explored in trauma and breaking up with busy. Imagine being in a glass snow globe and a toddler picking it up and shaking it with all her might. That's what life felt like.

Yet I wouldn't trade it for the world. Question everything. Learning happens everywhere—for you *and* for your daughter. It's not limited to the four walls we know as school. In fact, I believe very little of it actually happens there.

It's up to you, Mom, to create the environments and maximize the opportunities for the learning to happen. Trust your gut. Remember, you are the expert when it comes to your daughter. And don't let anyone ever convince you otherwise.

THE PATH TO MAGIC

1. How do my moments of feeling jealousy serve as clues to my innermost longings?

2. Who are others with whom I can explore nontraditional opportunities for learning?

3. What is our family's philosophy, and how can we bring our schooling into alignment with that philosophy?

4. What is my daughter's passion or calling? Thinking outside of the box, what would be an effective path of education to pursue?

CHAPTER FIFTEEN

Traditions

"Don't be afraid of being different; be afraid of being the same as everyone else."

—ANONYMOUS

Live differently. If you want a life like no one else, you have to live in a way that's different than everyone else. Status quo just won't suit you. It certainly doesn't suit the way our family wants to be.

We prefer countercultural and unconventional living. If everyone is going right, we'll go left. Not for the sake of being different, but because we realize the masses don't have it all figured out. In fact, it's usually the blind leading the blind. If you asked the crowd why they are going in a particular direction, they'll likely say, "Because everyone else is doing it." That doesn't work for me. And if you're reading this book, I bet you're starting to ask yourself more questions about what you want, why you want it, and what new ideas are needed for moving toward the life you want to have. It's time to forge a new path.

NEW OPPORTUNITIES

We tend to underestimate what our girls are capable of. What if we adopted the mindset that we are raising adults—*not* little girls?

Our daughters grow into the conversations we have around them.

What kind of conversations are they exposed to? What would happen if you put them in rooms with other adults who validate the lessons you want them to learn? Does it really matter where they get their ideas as long as they get them? We get to stack the deck in our favor by placing our daughters in the environments we want them to be in.

I call this a smart use of leverage. What would happen if we simply leveraged all of the opportunities that already exist around us to raise daughters who think in a new entrepreneurial fashion?

The number of times our girls have heard things like, "I wish my parents had taken me to things like this when I was your age," or, "You have no idea how old I was when I heard this stuff for the first time… You have no idea how lucky you are." What do you think happens when they hear things like this over and over and over again? It doesn't matter where they get their new ideas as long as they get them. Stack the deck in her favor.

NEW QUESTIONS, NEW TRADITIONS

Our decision to start exposing our girls to new ways of exploration and learning started by asking new questions. It began to open our eyes to how we could impact the girls—and our entire family—by changing our perspective and getting us out of the rut of status quo.

In order to live differently, you'll need to start crafting a new way of living.

Let's explore some questions you and your daughter can start asking together to build a life that supports the new directions in which you want to move. Following each question, I'll share some answers that worked for our family.

> **Who are my people? What communities and groups will support us in asking new questions, thinking differently, and living a life by design?**

- We sought out new communities where we were most definitely *not* the smartest people in the room. These included real estate specific communities, educational courses such as The Landmark Forum, Tony Robbins, The Empowerment Partnership (Neurolinguistic Programming), and Gary Keller's Quantum Leap for Kids. It also meant finding families who were interested in thinking differently as well. These families were key in leading us to new opportunities.
- Create individual and family bucket lists and post them in visible spaces. Find other families and friends who will

do this with you. Make it a race to get to a hundred items on each list as quickly as possible. Just by creating the lists, you'll open up new conversations and spark the opportunity for curiosity and inquiry. By sharing your lists with others, you will increase the probability of achieving items through the accountability. This will also allow you to help others by connecting them with opportunities of which you may be aware, and vice versa.

How can we create a home environment that supports living differently?

- Start a gratitude wall or jar. I have yet to meet a mom who thinks, *Hey! I want to raise an entitled brat!* No one wants to be the mom with "that kid." You know exactly who I'm talking about. The girl who perhaps is wearing all of the latest fashions, goes on all the fancy trips, yet complains *all* the time. Nothing is ever good enough, nice enough, fast enough… the one who complains about the service. The antidote to this is simply gratitude. We can't hold feelings of gratitude and entitlement at the same time. Cultivating gratitude is a muscle that, when used, will simply grow and get stronger.
- Have her write thank you notes on a weekly basis to someone she is grateful for. This is a way to express gratitude and cultivate that muscle while also teaching her how to appropriately write a note. Better yet, do this together every week at a designated time. You'll both benefit.
- Start a weekly family meeting. We have meetings all the time in our work settings. What if we ran our family in a similar fashion and held family meetings to discuss our dreams, goals, and plans? Weekly meetings are a way we

can have accountability and measure incremental progress to our destination.

What can we incorporate into our traditional school routines?

- Particularly when our girls were in traditional school, I wanted to make sure they never received the perfect attendance award. I always felt sad for the kid who got it. Did your parents ever pull you out to do something fun and silly? I would pretend like we were driving to school and instead surprise them with a trip to an amusement park for the day. Hersheypark in Pennsylvania was our happy place for a quick day trip adventure!
- Pull her out for lunch unannounced or join her for lunch at school if possible.
- Bring in a treat for the whole class, just because. Shop for the treat together and write affirmations or a note to give to each classmate. Everyone wins when we encourage our neighbor.

What communities can we create to help others experience a little bit of living differently?

- Our girls have grown up watching us host parties. We thoroughly enjoy bringing people together for the sake of growing community. If you are going to have people over, host parties with a purpose. One idea is to host a "Come as you will be" party. Invite friends to come to the party as who they *will be* in five years! Roll out the red carpet and have the attendees articulate who they will be in five years—as if it has already happened.

- Thanks to our friends, Jimmy and Ivelisse Page, we adopted the concept of choosing "One Word" as a mantra for the year. To learn more about this, pick up Jimmy's book, *One Word that Will Change Your Life*. Every person in our family has picked a word for the past seven years. On New Year's Day, we gather together and paint our individual words on small canvases so we can hang them up in our kitchen. As we see the word show up in each other's lives, we call it out! We have since started inviting other families to join us every year in our backyard.
- Create vision boards. Grab magazines or print pictures and words from the internet. Start envisioning what you want life to look like and put it on a board with a glue stick! Us adults really need to do more of these crafty projects to bring out the kid in us. The conversations that ensue because of the words or pictures we choose are priceless. Perhaps also do a family vision board to include everyone together and represent all of the things your family stands for in the world.

How can we help our daughters understand money and investing?

- The number one topic people wish their parents had taught them more about at home is money. We can learn a lot about our daughters' predispositions to money when we watch how they react to having their own and being able to make decisions about how to use it. Wouldn't you rather your daughter learn to save, spend, and give while she's living at home? Get her a debit card as early as possible. Teach her these principles now. Use a card such as

Greenlight, which has an app associated with it so you can maintain some basic controls, depending on her age.
- Buy stocks as a family. Have your daughter do research on which ones to buy and have her defend her answer. Buy small amounts of stock and have her report back weekly on changes to the market.
- Do a pro forma on your current house. If she were buying it today, what would it cost? How much are property taxes? How could it be financed? How would she know if it was a good investment?

What tasks traditionally completed by Mom are our daughters completely capable of doing themselves?

When we explored this question, my mind practically exploded with the number of things we rob our daughters of doing, thereby stunting their growth and learning. Consider some of the following:

- Filling out forms in the doctor's office
- Handling self-checkout at the grocery store
- Writing out the invitations for their birthday party (or creating and setting up her electronic invitation)
- Meal planning
- Researching recipes and making the shopping list
- Comparing prices on a product she wants to buy
- Writing out the check for you to sign / paying the bills and addressing the envelope
- Creating spreadsheets for the household budget
- Packing her own lunch (ours started at five years old)
- Doing her own laundry

Disclaimer: All of these things will take more time when she does them. Patience is required. Know that the greatest learning comes from her *doing* the work while you watch and guide as needed. Think about all the skills you want her to have when she leaves home. The time to teach it? Now. You don't have as long as you think.

How can we make family vacations purposeful?

- Before the trip starts, pick some words that describe how you all want the trip to go. Incorporate it into a declarative sentence that is memorable, short, and repeatable. Something like, "We have fun and adventure no matter what!"
- Have your daughter do the trip planning. Create spreadsheets together, and have her find ticket dates, prices, and hotel costs and options. Have her set up a budget for the trip and include all items that would need to be accounted for such as meals, souvenirs, and rental cars. Have her investigate possible itineraries and excursion opportunities.

As a business owner, how can I leverage the power of my business to help my daughter grow?

- Get her business cards, *now*! Our girls had their own business cards, which looked exactly like ours along with the title of Marketing Assistant. They knew that if they found someone who wanted to buy or sell a home with us, they would make a hundred dollars upon completion of the sale. The girls would put their cards on bulletin boards and would have conversations with friends they

would not have had otherwise. Business cards are tied to identity. If they believe they are an entrepreneur, they will show up accordingly in the world.
- Have your daughter make phone calls to check in with your clients just to check in as a customer service representative would. Give her a script to follow and coach her along the way. Our girls started doing this at age eleven. Clients love hearing from young entrepreneurs!

How can I expose her directly to owning a business?

- Help her start a business today! I love supporting a budding entrepreneur, and I believe most people feel the same way. An easy way to begin is to participate in a local Children's Business Fair in your area (visit www.ChildrensBusinessFair.org). Start by just attending to observe or dive right in as a participant! YouTube has an endless supply of business ideas for young entrepreneurs. Our girls have made everything from dishwasher cleaning pods ("Pods from the Gods"), which won Lorra one hundred dollars at our local business fair, to homemade cake pops, to facial scrubs and even just store-bought water bottles to resell.
- Have her explore opportunities to do an apprenticeship for a career or passion that intrigues her. You'd be surprised how many business owners will say yes to this opportunity! If your daughter loves to bake, do interior design, real estate investing, medicine, actuarial science—opportunity is everywhere. Allow her to network to find opportunities that will help her uncover if she wants to pursue the passion farther or perhaps a different path.

Knowing what you *don't* want in this case is just as valuable as knowing what you *do* want.

Opportunity is everywhere. This is perhaps one of the greatest lessons you can help your daughter uncover through just these few ideas. Blow out the boundaries. Your life doesn't need to look like everyone else's. Exploring what makes you uniquely you and pursuing this new pathway is the ultimate key to unlocking a life of freedom and joy. You only get one life, Mom. So start asking some new questions and living in a way that aligns with what matters most to you.

THE PATH TO MAGIC:
1. Thinking back to my own childhood, what things do I wish had been different? How can I use these desires to create something new for my family today?

2. How can we create conversations in our family to build our own countercultural traditions?

3. We each have the opportunity to live our legacy every day. What legacy do I want to live and eventually leave for my daughter? How can I create traditions to support my legacy?

CHAPTER SIXTEEN

Change

"Growth is painful. Change is painful. But nothing is as painful as staying stuck somewhere you don't belong."
—MANDY HALE

I'm a rebel. So rebellious, in fact, I did something unthinkable when I was seventeen and just two months away from high school graduation. From birth until the age of seventeen years old, my legal first name was Alice.

In a sea full of Jennifers and Emilys, I really dreaded how old the name Alice sounded. The only Alice people knew were old grandmothers or the 1980s television sitcom featuring Alice the waitress at Mel's Diner.

Although I rarely remember my dreams come morning, I had a vivid dream once that I was taking a test in school. I was writing my name on the top of the test, and I wrote Alycen, which was a name I really loved. It had a unique spelling, and something about it brought me such joy. After waking up from the dream, it all felt so real. I wanted more than anything to change my name from Alice to Alycen, but I knew my dad would be less than pleased. I was after all named for my grandmother, who also happened to pass away on the other side of the world the same day I was born.

But then I thought, *What if I just changed it by one letter instead and went from an "I" to a "Y"?*

So there you have my high school rebellion. I was a really good kid who loved going to church youth group, and my biggest rebellion was that I changed my name from Alice with an "I" to Alyce with a "Y". But there's something about this reinvention that every human soul craves. I was excited about being able to go into a new college environment and reinvent myself. No one knew me for being a certain way, so it felt like a do-over in the best of ways.

There are lots of opportunities for reinvention throughout life, whether it's going to a new school, going to college, or perhaps making a geographic move. But after settling down as a mom, however, it can sometimes be tough to break out of a routine to find these opportunities to reinvent. A lack of reinvention or change can breed stagnation and lead to a loss of hope. Reinvention is a necessary part of growth and change.

SEASONS

College was a monetarily expensive social experiment. I took a whole bunch of classes, which I don't really remember, stayed up really late writing papers, and made lots of friends. My faith in God grew deeper and more solid.

The single most important thing I learned, however, came in a class taught by Dr. Carla Waterman in Spring of my junior year. She talked about the concept of seasons.

While we are in school, semesters form artificial seasons. If we're having a bad semester, we can see exactly when the semester will end and when we'll have the opportunity for a fresh start. Our seasons are predetermined and predictable. Many of us live in this world of artificial seasons for at least eighteen years, if not until twenty-two upon college graduation.

Once we leave the world of academia, however, the seasons become blurry and hard to distinguish. No one tells us, ahead of time, how long the next season will be.

For me, that was jarring.

How long would I be working that dreaded filing job? Would I die doing this seemingly menial work?

How long would I go without finding my tribe—my people? Would I feel alone forever?

How long would we live in the same place?

How long would I drive the same car?

How long before having kids?

The answer to all of these questions felt the same to me: *Forever*. Is this how it all ends?

And, of course, it isn't true. The problem is that the seasons aren't predefined, so we tend to not recognize the seasons until *after* they've already changed. No cute little predetermined three-month semesters in real life, friends.

One thing we can be sure of is seasons are *always* in play and *always* changing, whether we *feel* them or not. If we're in a bad time, we can take solace in knowing, "This, too, shall pass."

In good times, we should also realize, "This, too, shall pass."

FEELING BURIED
You are one decision, one relationship, one conversation, one moment, one choice, one introduction away from having a totally different life. Henry David Thoreau stated, "Most people live lives of quiet desperation." You don't have to be one of those people.

If you're feeling like you've been buried by life and some days close to six feet under, consider if, instead, you're a seed. The transformed focus of realizing that you have been planted can help you be patient with yourself.

Chinese bamboo trees, when first planted, show no signs of growth on the surface despite being nurtured and cared for—for the period of *four years*. Typically, in year five or so, the first signs of sprouts appear, and within just six months the bamboo grows upward of one hundred feet—in a month! That's over three feet *per day*.

So what's happening in the five years where there is no apparent movement at all?

The roots are forming and developing a foundational system to handle the upcoming growth ahead. Change is coming. It's inevitable. We just won't see the season change until after it's happened in most cases.

If you're feeling a bit buried, consider that you might be the strong mighty bamboo tree—firmly planted, growing your foundation and roots, and ready to sprout in the right time and season.

LIVE YOUR DREAM AND HELP SOMEONE ELSE

A few years ago, I had asked my friend, Wendy, if we could meet while I was visiting her hometown of Austin. I was wanting to make some big life changes and wasn't sure how to make them happen. Like any great coach, she asked me some questions to help me get clarity on what mattered most.

I was so conflicted at that time. The life I wanted seemed so different than the life I had in front of me. I knew I would regret not doing something about it, however, and I knew I didn't want to get to the end of my life and regret not even trying. I was scared of what other people would think of me and what they would say.

I had built a life that looked pretty awesome from the outside. We had the American dream, and I was ready to blow all of it up. I couldn't describe why, yet I just knew it didn't feel right.

I had been living according to the societal script and realized I hadn't been able to hear my own voice in the midst of it all.

I wanted to live in warm weather. I wanted a school for our kids that we loved. I wanted to love where I lived. I wanted to be outside more. I wanted more community. I wanted a slower pace of life.

I remember asking Wendy, "What will I say to people when they ask about the changes?" I was deeply fearful of what people would think. I was fearful about trying to make these changes and failing. Without skipping a beat, she said something that has become a mantra for me, something that resonated deep in my soul and instantly brought freedom.

She said, "You just tell them that you're living your dream and you want to help them live theirs too."

When I shifted my focus from it being about me to instead being about all the women I could help be a role model for, a fire lit inside me. I realized in that moment I could help liberate others who were living in the same hamster wheel I had created for myself. No one was coming to rescue me. If I wanted to live a life I loved, I just had to go do it. The world has us hypnotized. Grade school, college, job, marriage, kids, invest in the stock market, go on vacation once a year. Asking different questions helped me to wake up to my own life to bring about change such as moving from Baltimore to Austin, shifting career paths, building new communities, and living life more on my own terms to be congruent with my dreams.

Change doesn't happen overnight, but it also doesn't happen by staying still. First, you need clarity on what you want. How vivid is your vision for the future? Don't worry about the "how" for now. Just dream. If life could look any way you wanted it, describe it in the clearest detail you can. Talk it through with a friend or a coach, journal it, create a vision board. It will continue to evolve and grow. It won't happen by accident, however. Set an intention and create the space to be able to dream the dreams that you've perhaps buried away as I had.

I'm really excited to be able to say I'm living out my dream today. And part of my dream is helping other women live theirs out too. That includes you, Mom. I want to help you live out your dream too. And as you live yours out, your daughter will be inspired to create and live out hers.

Life is too short to *not* live your dreams. Let's make some moves in the direction of the life you want right now, Mom. We can do this together. Others are counting on you. Your daughter is first in line.

THE PATH TO MAGIC

1. What are three things about my life I enjoy?

2. If I could change one or two things in my life, what would they be?

3. What questions have I been afraid to ask myself about my own future?

4. What activity can I do with my daughter to explore our dreams together?

5. How will my choices to live my dream inspire my daughter? Who else might they inspire?

PART FIVE:

COACH

"If you don't like the road you're walking, start paving another one."

—DOLLY PARTON

In my favorite movie, *The Greatest Showman*, the stunningly gorgeous Zendaya plays the role of Anne Wheeler, a brilliant trapeze artist. Because I have a fear of heights and despise the feeling of falling, you'll never find me remotely near an actual trapeze. The trust, faith, and strength one must have to perform such a feat is extraordinary.

A trapeze artist has this moment of seemingly blind faith when she has to let go of the bar and simply trust something (or someone) else will be there to grab onto when she's mid-air. There is a split-second moment when she is suspended in air—arms raised high in anticipation—yet nothing is present but wide-open air and the intense pull of gravity. When I watch her, it looks like it is only for a split second where she is suspended. But I can imagine it may feel like an eternity while waiting and trusting that the trapeze bar will be there to catch—and that she'll have the strength and capability to seize it when it arrives.

That's pretty much what it feels like to be entrepreneurial and have an entrepreneurial spirit. It is trusting that even though you're holding on to something good, something else is calling you that you are compelled to go to. A risk calls your name. An adventure and a calling that only you can fulfill. But in order to get there, you have to be willing to let go and take the risk that there might not be a bar to catch—that the adventure may not look the way you assumed it would. Or, you might just fall into the net below—if there is one. If there is a net, you may need to bounce off of it and climb that ladder again to grab a hold of what you know and then try all over again.

Yet to have the willingness to take that initial risk of letting go of something good for something great is the very essence of the entrepreneurial spirit.

The call to adventure is exhilarating and compels us to go beyond our natural boundaries.

These risks could come in many forms: Take the job or start a business? Get into this relationship or wait? Move or bloom where you're planted? Pursue formal education or take an unconventional path? Invest in real estate or pay off some debt?

All of these questions are reasons why we need an outside perspective. The trapeze artist doesn't decide one day to perform a death-defying feat. Instead, she has a coach to help give guidance, support, and insight. The roles of a coach are many—to help create vision, to inspire, to uncover blind spots, and to ultimately unlock the potential of the player to maximize performance.

Mom, your daughter is getting ready to grab the trapeze in this game called life. It's your job to let her go do her thing and to act as her coach along the way. Some days she'll bounce off the net below, and you get to encourage her to climb back up the ladder. Other days, she'll perform flawlessly. Regardless, you can't do it for her, but you can ramp up your skills to be the best coach possible for her. And, in the process, you'll benefit from having your own coach too.

THE HERO'S JOURNEY
One of the reasons we love the school our daughters attend is because of their underlying belief in Joseph Campbell's Hero's Journey framework, which allows for a robust, learner-driven community. In its most simplistic explanation, the hero's journey consists of three main parts: a call to adventure, tests and trials, and the return back home. If you watch any good movie, you'll see this simple pattern play out. Pick

any Disney movie you've watched with your daughter and you'll easily pull out these pieces. The main character in the story is always the hero, yet somewhere in the adventure, usually during the tests and trials, the hero encounters both an obstacle and a guide.

HERO'S JOURNEY

RETURN
The hero returns in triumph to the familiar world - with new knowledge and insight on a higher plane to help lift up others.

DEPARTURE
The hero leaves the ordinary world behind to follow a calling.

INITIATION
The hero ventures into the unknown and overcomes various obstacles and challenges - answering the call to adventure.

There are three simple and distinct acts within the hero's (dare I say *"shero's"*?) journey:

1. Departure—The hero leaves the ordinary world behind to follow a calling.
2. Initiation—The hero ventures into the unknown and overcomes various obstacles and challenges, answering the call to adventure.

3. Return—The hero returns in triumph to the familiar world with new knowledge and insight on a higher plane to help lift up others.

Responding to the hero's journey's "call to adventure" requires passion, curiosity, and a calling. Because the journey will be a new one outside the boundaries of what has been comfortable and known, the hero will need help. The inevitable trial of the journey will require a guide. Everything changes when you allow a trusted outside perspective to come into your adventure as your guide.

As we'll talk about in the following chapters, guides come in different flavors: coaches, mentors, and consultants. Knowing the difference and being purposeful in how you show up in your guidance role will be vital to your daughter's development and growth.

In the next few chapters, we'll look at the different roles of a coach, a consultant, and a mentor, and how all three are important and necessary. Along the journey, we will encounter failures and setbacks. How we view failure and coach our daughters through it is crucial. And finally, we'll look at how to continue to fully equip you, Mom, with everything you need to keep growing so you can be your absolute best for yourself and your daughter. It's never too late to live a life you love—and to teach your daughter to do the same. You've got this, Coach!

CHAPTER EIGHTEEN

Roles

"Where her thoughts ended and mine began remain a mystery. I have said her words so often that I now wonder if they are my own."

—HELEN KELLER (ABOUT HER MENTOR, ANNE SULLIVAN)

Mentor, consultant, coach. We tend to hear these words interchangeably in conversation. We find a great deal of overlap between how each of these roles function, yet it is critical to understand the differences so we know when to employ each role in our own lives or in the lives of our girls.

MENTOR

Mentors are people who have already done something we want to do or think we might want to do. You'll find that we can look for mentors who have been successful in areas of health, finance, or career, for example. Mentors are people who have gone before us, achieved some levels of success, and generously share their journey with us. They are people who want to give back by sharing their own experience.

Mentor programs start early. You can find them in schools where high schoolers mentor elementary students. They're able to do this because they just have a little more life experience. The only requirements to be a mentor are to be one or two steps ahead on the path and to be willing to give your time. I've been honored to serve as a mentor for various high school- and college-aged women interested in pursuing entrepreneurship over the years. They come to shadow my work and ask questions about my path.

Mentors have been highly valuable in my life. I didn't even realize I sought out mentors at a young age. I was just looking for help to survive! Who do I know who can help me? As a first generation American, I needed someone to mentor me so I had insight on how to navigate my schooling. I needed mentors to tell me how to handle money. I needed mentors to help me with marriage. Mentors can be found just about anywhere if you're looking for them. Mentors share what they did that works and things that perhaps didn't go as planned and areas that, with some hindsight, they may have approached differently. As a mentor, there's a feeling of, "If I had only known this when I was at your stage, here's what I might've done differently."

What mentors do not necessarily offer, however, is a system of how they got where they are. Instead, mentors offer their own personalized stories of "here's how I got to where I am now." Mentors have very little expectation that you will achieve what they've achieved. They are merely sharing their story in hopes it will be beneficial for you. Mentors typically mentor others for free. They offer their own personal life experience—nothing more, nothing less.

We have encouraged our girls to find mentors everywhere they can. If they show an interest, we encourage them to pursue it by asking questions. Mentors don't have to be formal relationships, and in most cases they aren't. Annika started asking me questions about what her friend's parents did for a living that they were able to travel so much. Instead of feeding her the answers I knew, I encouraged her to go find out for herself. Empower your daughter to seek out the answers by following her own curiosity. Many mentors will come in the form of other parents and trusted professionals in your community.

CONSULTANT

Consultants, on the other hand, are people we bring in from the outside to give us strategy. We hire consultants to give recommendations and to tell us what to do. Consultants analyze our situations and play out different scenarios. They give us various options based on their findings and expertise. When I worked in the corporate world, it was common to hire outside consultants for perspective. It was ultimately up to us as the hiring party to decide whether to heed the consultant's advice or not.

At times in our entrepreneurial business life, we have brought in marketing consultants to tell us what to do in areas where we were clueless. As a real estate professional, I love seeing aesthetically beautiful things, but my gift is not in creating the beauty. So, I'd often hire consultants to come in with their professional advice. Consultants get paid for their time and their knowledge. Consultants have all kinds of tools in their tool belt, and they whip out the right ones based on your individual situation. And again, like the mentor, the consultant doesn't have much of a vested interest in whether you succeed. They've been brought in to do a job, they do it, and then they leave. Consultants usually work on an hourly or per project basis. If they perform well, they may be called back in the future when help is needed.

Consultant is the role I'm honored to play with our oldest daughter, Karissa, now that she's an adult and has moved away from home. She doesn't always need me, but at times she'll choose to call for advice. She may or may not take my advice, and that's completely her choice. Whether or not we're in alignment on what she decides to do largely depends on how I handled the first eighteen years as her coach.

COACH
Coaches have a true vested interest in the game being played. They want the player to win because when the player wins, they all win. Coaches teach players how to think by asking hard questions and allowing self-discovery to take place. Often times, the player borrows confidence from the coach when they have low confidence in themselves.

Coaches sometimes call the play, and at other times, they allow the player to call the play. Coaches don't do the work for the players, but they help them think through strategies and decisions. The best of coaches are both loved and respected—yet, not always liked. (Have you ever not been liked by your daughter? Me too, sister.) The coach cares deeply about the player and the team winning the overall game.

Every one of the world's best, in any field, has a coach. The best athletes, the best business people, the best in *any* industry, are wise enough to enlist the help of a coach. The highest performers have coaches in the best of seasons and on the worst and toughest of days. And the crazy thing is, the coaches haven't necessarily done what they're coaching their clients to do. They do, however, possess the skills to unlock the potential that's inside. And once the potential is unlocked, the possibilities for the player are endless.

Coaches are skilled at seeing the potential and bringing out the best in others.

They are empathic listeners, they help set goals to achieve desired outcomes, they are genuinely curious and skilled in asking great questions, and they give honest feedback and perspective. They help the player discover for herself the best path forward by reflecting back what they observe. A great coach sees more in the player than the player can see in herself.

Coaches aren't usually up in the limelight. They act as a guide to the hero in the story. Do you know the name Bob Bowman? Most people don't, yet he coached Michael Phelps, who won twenty-three Olympic gold medals. Phelps also won five other Olympic medals in addition to the twenty-three gold ones, for those of my hometown Baltimore friends who are keeping score!

Being a great coach is the role you'll play as a mom for most of the first eighteen years of life. If we've done well in those eighteen years, our daughter will call us in as a consultant as she navigates through adulthood. Becoming your daughter's coach and garnering her love and respect during the first eighteen years will determine the role she will want you to play in the future.

How will you use these precious years as a coach to your daughter? It's not uncommon to doubt our own abilities and defer to the thoughts and opinions of others. However, I know with certainty that

> ***You are the best coach for your daughter, as God would not have given you your daughter if you were not.***

You were handpicked for her for such a time as this. Coaches help players maximize their potential. Isn't that what we aim to do every single day as moms?

What is needed for you to step into this identity as a coach? Some of us have never thought of this as one of the hats we wear. Coaches inspire and bring out the best in their players. Maybe you desire to do this for your daughter yet struggle with knowing how. If that's the case, you're simply ill-equipped, and that is easily remedied. Own this part of your role as mom and become the coach she needs. Teach her how to create the life she wants by modeling, affirming, giving grace, and inquiring. You have everything you need to draw out the immense potential that lies within her.

If you believe that you can listen well to your daughter, that you can help her set goals to achieve *her* desired outcomes (not yours), that you can be inquisitive and curious without judgment, and that you can create a psychologically safe space for two-way feedback, you'll be well-equipped as her coach.

SO NOW THAT I KNOW THE DIFFERENCE, WHAT DO I DO?
First, we take care of you, Mom. Put on your own oxygen mask first. Get a coach for yourself in whatever area you need. Allow this coach to serve as a model for you. You might need a physical coach, a financial coach, a Mom coach, a spiritual coach, a business coach, or an overall life coach. What area in your life are you wanting to improve right now? Get a coach in that area, and you'll learn skills to become a better coach yourself to bring your daughter along.

Taking care of yourself first requires creating margin and the willingness to take a long hard look in the mirror. A great coach will act as a mirror for you, reflecting back what they see, so you can pursue growth in areas of your choosing. A coach will create a space for you to get back to your authentic self so you can build on the gifts that already reside within you waiting to be unleashed.

In order to do this, it is important to find your baseline. A great tool for this is our LYFEwheel resource, which you can access for free as a part of the MAGIC Momhood community (www.TheMAGICMom.com). This resource will allow you to take an honest look at areas of your life where you're thriving and others where even a slight shift will allow you to create the momentum you need to grow.

As your daughter's head coach, you will help her see the opportunities all around her. Encourage your daughter to find other voices who will serve as the voice of a mentor, consultant, and coach. It takes the whole village, so embrace the community around you and don't go at this alone.

THE PATH TO MAGIC:
1. Which characteristics of a great coach—such as asking questions that promote self-discovery, being nonjudgmental, instilling confidence, or helping to find and use outside resources—am I already embodying for my daughter?

2. Imagine engaging a coach in an area of your own life. What could that make possible?

3. Who are the mentors, consultants, and coaches available to me and my daughter today?

4. What is one way my coaching has adapted to my daughter's needs as she grows older? Is there another area of my coaching that needs to change and adapt to a new season of her life?

CHAPTER NINETEEN

Failure

"It is impossible to live without failing at something, unless you live so cautiously that you might as well not have lived at all, in which case you have failed by default."

—JK ROWLING

The best success stories start with failure.

When Lorra was in seventh grade, she decided to run for student government. She took in donuts for the class. She made the world's most hysterical, laugh-out-loud funny campaign posters. They were so funny, in fact, I posted them on social media for my friends to see. The post was among my top five as my friend circles responded enthusiastically to a seventh-grade campaign because of the creativity and marketing savvy of a twelve-year-old.

When I came home on election day, I was excited to find out how it had played out. She gave it her all, no doubt. She's a bit of ham, so when I looked her in the eyes and she didn't reply, I wondered if she was just keeping me in suspense.

And then the tears started quietly flowing.

She had lost the seventh-grade election. It's quite a big deal when you're twelve and it's your whole world.

I was angry and confused. How in the world did she lose? Her marketing and posters were sheer genius.

As her coach, however, I knew how important this moment was. This was the perfect opportunity for me to either drown in all the emotions or help her steer her experience of failure to higher ground.

I kept my composure and first asked about her feelings. She was obviously sad. She wanted it so badly. I wanted it so badly *for her*. But it wasn't the path. While expressing empathy and being with her, I was communicating that this event was not her identity.

She then said these words, which I will never forget: "Mom, I'm really sad and disappointed. But it's okay. Failure is a part of my story, and it'll be in my book one day. This all needed to happen so I have a story to tell others."

The wisdom she spouted out effortlessly wasn't lost on me. Failure *is* the best of teachers if we allow it to be. In the movie *Rocky*, the main character says, "It ain't how hard you can hit. It's how hard you can get hit and keep moving forward." Lorra got hit hard and made a decision in that moment to keep moving forward.

What is *your* relationship with failure, Mom? Do you run toward it and welcome it—for yourself and for your daughter? Or do you do everything in your power to avoid it in order to maintain an image or not risk the feeling of disappointment?

The truly successful understand that:

> *Failure isn't just a part of growth.*
> *Failure is instead the cause of growth.*

Without failure, our rate of growth would be lessened. If we want to grow faster, we *must* fail faster.

As a coach to our daughters, one of the greatest gifts we can offer them is a safe space to experience failures. I would rather she learn to fail while she has me standing by as her coach to encourage, guide, and inspire her along the way. The alternative is that she experiences the inevitabilities of failure only *after* she leaves home and without a clue as to how to frame it.

As tennis superstar Serena Williams brilliantly states, "I've grown most not from victories, but setbacks. If winning is God's reward, losing is how he teaches us."

The best coaches like you, Mom, model how to glean the lessons along the way.

MILLION-DOLLAR IDEAS

We all have a million-dollar idea inside of us. In Sara Blakely's case, all she wanted to do was wear white pants to a party without visible underwear lines. With $5,000 and a dream in her basement, Spanx was born. In 2012, she was crowned by *Forbes* as the youngest self-made billionaire. The end.

These are the glamorous parts of the story and the ones we all seem to remember best. But the stories *behind* the story are what we should be studying. Because that's where all the MAGIC is.

Blakely initially wanted to be an attorney like her father, so she took the LSAT and failed. She studied her tail off a second time and did one point worse.

She then took a job at Disney World where she wanted to be Goofy. But they told her she was too short for the role and offered her the Chipmunk, which she declined.

For seven years, she sold fax machines door to door. Some of you reading this have probably never seen or used one, but they used to be on the cutting edge of tech! She cold-called all day and experienced rejection repeatedly.

Blakely's incredible relationship with failure was modeled for her at home, by her dad. When the Blakely kids were at the dinner table, he would ask them, "What did you fail at this week?"

Great coaches ask great questions. And that is a magnificent one.

Blakely's dad would be disappointed if they had nothing to share. On the contrary, he'd high-five and celebrate when Sara would tell him that she'd auditioned for a role and bombed it!

He knew people are paralyzed by the fear of failure. "My father wanted us to try everything and feel free to push the envelope. His attitude taught me to define failure as not trying something I want to do instead of not achieving the right outcome."

Behind every incident of failure is an opportunity or lesson—or, as Blakely puts it, "a chance to build your character." Spanx wouldn't have existed if she didn't fail the LSAT, twice.

You have a million-dollar idea inside of you. Your daughter has one inside of her. How many times as her coach will you encourage her to fail forward until she discovers it? Have you ever had that moment when you see a product or service you thought about years ago? Someone else just acted on it. That's the only difference between you and them. They were willing to try and fail while others were not.

Great coaches help their players run toward the failure—because they know that's where the greatest wins happen.

CHOOSE WHERE YOU WILL FAIL
Failure is a part of life, and it's a massive part of motherhood. Raising a daughter isn't like buying Ikea furniture with directions and little tools. No one gave me a manual when I left the hospital with any of my girls. Not to mention, each one of

my girls, with the same two parents growing up in the same home, are radically different from one another.

I used to be fearful of what I would do or say that would eventually land my daughter in therapy. "Am I doing this right? Am I doing this well enough? But look at how this other mom is doing it. That doesn't look anything like what I'm doing, so I must be doing it wrong."

I would make myself paranoid that I didn't enroll them in the right playgroup or the right class that would teach them to read by the time they were a year old.

I tried that kind of fearful, perfectionistic, paranoid mothering for a long, long while. And, quite frankly, it stinks. It's exhausting and draining. There is another way, however…

Choose your failure.

Good coaches know where they excel and where they need support. Coaches aren't isolated. They bring in a team around them to coach to areas where they aren't as strong. You can do the same, Mom. Build your team.

The more quickly we can accept that failure is a part of life and a part of motherhood, too, the better. You don't have to get all of it right.

First of all, acceptance that we won't be able to "do it all" is paramount. When in your life have you *ever* been able to do it all? This parenting gig is no exception. You can't do it all. And, if you can't do it all, how do you know which parts won't get done?

Either you need to decide what won't get done, or it will be decided for you by someone else. So my advice to you would be to *choose where you will fail.* Proactively decide it. Accept and come to peace with it.

Here are some examples of where I've decided to fail:

- At home, my laundry room will constantly be a mess. Everyone does their own laundry, and it's a disaster. I could choose to hire someone on my team to help in this area, or decide to fail at it and be at peace. I've chosen the latter in this season of life.

- My house will look lived in at all times. I'll express gratitude for having daughters who inhabit the space, but it will be a hot mess with things shoved in drawers and closets in the fifteen minutes before company arrives.

- My kids won't be eating gourmet food unless they learn to cook it themselves. Mom isn't gifted in the cooking arena, so fend for yourselves, chickadees. In different seasons, I've also built my team to include grocery delivery, meal subscription boxes, or even a college student to come food prep for the week.

- As the budget allows, I'll hire someone to help me with random household stuff, like returning

Amazon packages, wrapping presents, making doctor's appointments, and so, so much more.

Bottom line is this: I will proactively choose where I will fail. Prioritization is key. When you take a look at all of the things on your plate, what would you consider to be the top 20 percent that only *you* can do with and for your daughter? *Do those things.* Prioritize that 20 percent.

Could the other items on your list be completed by someone else 80 percent as well as you could do them? (Or in my case, with laundry and cooking, 500 percent times *better* than I ever could have done!) If someone else can do it 80 percent as well as you can, let them do it. This is called leveraging your time, SuperMom. You may not be able to do it all, but through the power of leverage, you'll be able to accomplish more for yourself and your family. And you will keep your sanity.

The best coaches build a high-functioning team. Become a master at building yours.

FAILURE EQUALS SUCCESS
Our failures are our greatest successes. When we boil down our success, they're just a pile of accumulated failures.

I grew up in a home where, if I came home with six A's and a B+, the first thing to be noticed was the B+. When you see the Liberty Bell, what do you notice? The crack. That's what it's famous for. What color is the pen that tells us which answers are incorrect on a test? Red. We are taught at a very young age even through pen color that failure is bad and something to be avoided.

Entrepreneurs, however, see failure entirely differently. Entrepreneurs see failure as one more way their current solution doesn't work and hold the belief that now they are one step closer to finding the right path.

Great coaches like you, Mom, will make failure something to celebrate as opposed to hanging their heads low in shame and defeat. A number of times I didn't win the client. Business Philosopher Jim Rohn says, "Don't wish it were easier, wish you were better." Failure is a signal to grow our skills. We just need to extend some grace to ourselves and others along the way. And don't worry—momhood will provide lots of opportunities for us to fail as moms and to coach our daughters through failure on the way. That's a guarantee.

THE PATH TO MAGIC:
1. What was modeled for me as a child about how to view failure?

2. What is my personal relationship with failure today?

3. How is my life better today because of some of the failures I've experienced? What does failing well look like?

4. How do I want to show up as a coach for my daughter when she encounters failure?

5. When I fail, or when things do not go as well as I'd hoped, how do I encourage myself?

CHAPTER TWENTY

Act

"You need to recognize that the risk of moving toward your dreams is much lower than the slow, everyday punishment you inflict on yourself by suppressing your dream."

—MEL ROBBINS

If you've made it this far, I know some things about you:

1. **You have some dreams. Big ones and little ones. Dreams for yourself and dreams for your daughter.**

Nurture those dreams for yourself first. If some of your dreams have died somewhere between changing diapers, running carpool, building your own business, and taking care of everyone else around you, it's time to reclaim some old ones and start dreaming new ones. But how?

Journal. Pick up a brand new one. Don't get one last written in years ago that's been sitting on your shelf since. Get a new one that you like. It's okay, it's preferable even, to get a really nice one and spend some money on it. You spend money on lots of other books. This one will be filled with your dreams, your thoughts, and your stories. If you'd spend twenty-five dollars on a hardcover book, spend at least that much on a journal that holds the road map to your life and future self. Also, get a great pen! One that flows well with which you enjoy writing. Many of my journals are filled with purple ink just because it brings me joy.

Once you get the journal, then what? This is where panic tends to set in. We tend to panic because we are doing something new. But you've done new things before, and you can do this. Pay attention to where you feel most alive. Do you prefer being in your favorite chair at home? Or do you prefer being in a coffee shop or out somewhere in nature? The right place to journal is the one where you feel most authentically yourself. This is all an experiment, so if it doesn't work out the first time, try somewhere different the next time. Just like Goldilocks, you'll know when it's just right for you.

When it comes time to write, one of my mentors taught me this structure that has served me well. Simply answer these three questions:

- What I did
- What I thought
- What I felt

Some days you might have little to say in these areas, and other days you may feel like you can't write fast enough. Draw pictures if you'd like. Doodle. Use colored pencils and fun markers. The only rule is this: There are no rules. This is about freeing up your mind and creating space for you to dream again. Space for you to remember that this life you're living isn't a dress rehearsal. It's the one and only shot you have. This is the place to create the life you *want* to live by design so you don't end up with regrets when it's time for the curtain to go down.

Helping your daughter with her dreams starts with you knowing and living yours.

Knowing and living yours starts with carving some space to re-engage with the authentic version of you—the little girl inside yourself.

2. **You know you're not currently living up to your full potential, but you are hell-bent on figuring out how to do it.**

You want to grow. You don't believe in staying stuck, yet you've found yourself there more often than you'd care to admit. You've become a slave to the day to day. Your routines are rock solid, and lots of people depend on you. You listen to a podcast here and there, read a few lines from the stack of books you've bought from Amazon that haunt you on your nightstand. You'll find the time to read them—one day. You have some audio books, too, and listen with one AirPod while you're figuring out how everyone in the house will eat dinner.

You know something has to give, but you can't figure out what. You are the glue that is holding everything together. You know there are others like you that seem to be living a life different and, in some ways, better than yours, and you want desperately to move in that direction.

If you only hear one thing, please hear my heart shouting this loudly right into yours:

> *It's never too late to live a life you love. And your daughter is counting on you to show her it's possible!*

3. **You don't want to do this alone.**

Taking the road less traveled means fewer opportunities to randomly bump into kind strangers on the journey. This isn't about introversion versus extroversion preferences, but rather having a group of people around to support you on your journey and help you see what you can't see—a group of fellow travelers who can celebrate your wins with you and who are experiencing the same pain with you.

A favorite quote in our home is:
"As we let our own light shine, we unconsciously give other people the permission to do the same. As we are liberated from our own fear, our presence automatically liberates others."
—MARIANNE WILLIAMSON

This is the power of a community. We literally liberate one another by being in community together. We need one another to continue these conversations. Our daughters who are being raised in these new ways with empowered MAGIC Moms need to be in community. You have the power to choose which communities will support and encourage you toward the life you want to live or default to the status quo.

All the knowledge I've shared with you in these pages from my journey is simply potential power. The *real* power is when you do something with it. I hope you choose to join other MAGIC Moms just like you virtually or in real life, and perhaps I'll get to hug you in real life one day soon.

We've had an incredibly fun ride to this point with our four girls, and we so look forward to all of the adventures that are still yet to come. We made lots of mistakes along the way and continue to lean into curiosity and wonder as our guides. When I sit back to look at the common thread behind all of the success we've had in fostering an entrepreneurial spirit within our girls, it all still boils down to some simple **MAGIC** that we can share together:

M (**Model**): How am I modeling who I want my daughter to be as an adult? Who is a model for me in this season?

A (**Affirm**): What affirmation can I speak aloud to allow my subconscious to help me find the answers I need?

G (**Grace**): Who can I extend grace to in this situation and moment?

I (**Inquire**): What new questions could I ask to open up more possibility?

C (**Coach**): How am I showing up as a coach to my daughter right now? Who is coaching me to become the best version of myself?

MAGIC Mom Manifesto

I am a MAGIC Mom.

I am the Mom of the perfect daughter for me.

I have big dreams inside of me waiting to be realized.

The greatest gift I pledge to give my daughter is to live an authentic and fully lived life.

I **model** the kind of person I want my daughter to be everyday and I commit to continuing on the journey of becoming.

I seek out models for myself from which to learn in order to become the person I want to be.

I **affirm** the beauty and character in myself and in my daughter everyday. I call out the good, knowing what I appreciate appreciates.

I give **grace** on the daily to myself and to my daughter. We make mistakes as it's the only way to grow.

I am a curious **inquisitor**. I ask powerful questions of myself and my daughter from a place of genuine curiosity and not one of judgment.

I actively seek out the **coach** I need in every area of my life. I am committed to being the best coach my daughter will ever need or know.

My second life has begun—recognizing now that I only have one.

It is never too late to live a life that I love.

I make MAGIC happen!

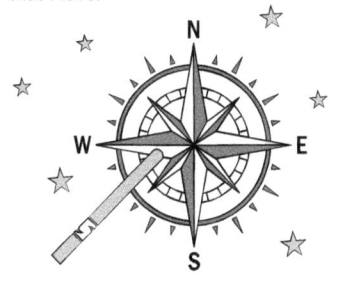

A Letter to You, Mom

"We are all just walking each other home."

—RAM DASS

Hey Sis,

At the end of the day, we're all just here together walking each other home. We're all doing our best to raise these young women so they will be strong leaders capable of living up to their full potential while being productive citizens of the world.

First, be sure to take care of yourself. More than anything, they need you to be around. That requires taking care of your physical, mental, and emotional health on all levels. If you'll get the oil changed on the car every three thousand miles, be sure to do the things that your wellbeing requires to be running strong.

It's okay to parent out of your own pain. Be the kind of mom you wish you had. Or if you were a lucky one, lean into the wonderful model your mom provided for you.

Create a vision for the relationship you want to have with your daughter. Don't leave it up to chance. Close your eyes and see what it looks like.

Take time to know your values. All of your decisions are based from this place, so understand what is driving your internal motor.

Anytime you hear yourself say, "But I'm supposed to..." immediately stop and respond with, "Says who?" and build from there. No one actually knows how it's supposed to go. Write your own script. It's never too late to live a life you love.

And last, come do this journey together with women who are experiencing the same joys and struggles.

Don't listen to me because I have it all figured out, because I assure you—I don't! Listen only because I am here on the journey too. I am here with you, willing to be vulnerable and to share as I cheer you on.

Find yourself a coach and a community, and go pay it forward. I look forward to seeing you over at www.TheMAGICMom.com and hearing *your* MAGIC story!

MAGICally yours,
Alyce

A Note to My Four Amazing Girls

- **Know what the "red tag" items are in life.**

The world is full of distractions. If you don't recognize and prioritize the "red tag" items, the world won't be of much help. The "red tag" items are the ones that will come with us to heaven on the other side of this temporal life. And crazy enough, there are only two items. The first is your relationship with Jesus. It's something you'll cultivate as you learn to hear His voice. I'm not talking about church or religion. Those are completely different. The relationship with Jesus is eternal. The second are the relationships with the people you bring with you to heaven. They'll have to find their own relationship with Him, but you get to be an earthly representation of Him wherever you go. Foster and nurture relationships. They'll be hard and hurt sometimes (a lot of times), but they are worth it.

- **Prioritize your health—physical and emotional.**

If we don't take care of our body, where will we live? Stay healthy for you and for those you love. Nourish your body with the right foods. Move your body every day and learn to love it. At the same time, remember that all of our actions are based on our emotions. Sharpen your skills in emotional fitness. Learn how to lead your heart and lead your emotions. I know we love a good Disney movie, but following your heart alone could lead to some ugly places. Emotions are not facts, so learning how to lead your heart is key.

- **Your playing small doesn't serve the world. By letting your light shine, you give others permission to do the same.**

I played small for a long time. I found my place by hiding in plain sight. When I started to get to know myself, I became really okay with who I wasn't. And once I could accept who I was and who I wasn't, I was just free to be me. I wish that for you too. Think about all the people on your journey who have inspired you to do some amazing things! You now have the responsibility to be that person for others. Go give other women permission to let their lights shine. The world needs as much light as it can possibly get. There's never too much.

- **Become highly skilled in noticing. So much about life is in noticing.**

In order to notice, you need to slow down, stop, and feel. Notice the things that bring you joy, and follow the breadcrumbs. Notice the things that break your heart. It will lead you to your purpose. When the tears come, pay attention. Your body doesn't lie. It's telling you something. Notice how you're feeling and what you're feeling. Notice if you're numbing your feelings with food, sleep, work, or social media. The world will tell you to hustle hard. There will be seasons of hustle, yet even in the hustle, your soul needs space to rest. By simply noticing, you'll create a path forward.

- **Read and write.**

The only difference between where you are today and five years from now are the people you let into your life—whether it be in real life, through reading their thoughts from books, or from writing your own books. Don't cheat yourself by consuming content only on social media. Get a journal and write about what you did, thought, and felt. The real learning comes from your own reflections of living your life.

- **Be a table builder.**

Women have been working so hard for a seat at the table for generations. Instead of fighting for a seat, just build more tables. Some women will be searching and yearning for a seat. Others will feel timid and undeserving and won't even know how to take up the space that was created for them. Be the one who creates the space for them to simply "be."

Everywhere you go, build tables and invite women to come sit with you. The world needs more tables and more seats. Some women will fight for seats because they believe they are scarce and limited. Show other women how to build tables too. Think abundantly and generously. Be known for creating space for women to be seen, heard, and known. The blessing you will receive in return will be far more than you could ever imagine possible.

- **Define what success looks like for you.**

Lots of people talk about success, but without defining it for yourself, it will never be achieved. The world will keep moving the goal posts, making it an unwinnable game. To me, success is defined as this:

"When the people who know me the best love me the most."

You know the good, the bad, and the ugly about me. And you choose to love me fiercely still. That's success in my book.

***

Know that I wrote this book with you four girls in mind. I didn't write it because I have all the answers. Rather, I pursued it because I wanted to follow my own curiosity. What worked in our home, and what didn't? What could we share with the world that would make relationships with mothers and daughters even more amazing? You girls are pure **MAGIC**—and my greatest joys.

I'm so honored to be the mom of four "bad donkeys." I hope this book gives you a little insight to see another side of me and of my deep love and admiration for each one of you—for who you are and who you are becoming.

Always treasure the sisterhood the four of you have. It is the most precious of gifts.

If you remember nothing else, remember these two things always:

I love you. And I'm *ridiculously* proud of you.

XO,
Mom

Acknowledgments

First, I give all my gratitude and love to my Heavenly Father. I got kind of a bum deal on the earthly father side of things, and I probably won't understand it this side of heaven. The good news is that I don't need to. Lord, you have given me exceedingly, abundantly more than I ever could have asked or imagined. I pray I'd be a good steward of your gifts and live a legacy that honors you above all else.

Seth, your DNA is literally all throughout these pages. Without the MAGIC Dad, the MAGIC Mom wouldn't exist. I am so crazy proud of this life we've created together. It's been joy-filled, adventurous and messy to say the least, and I wouldn't have it any other way. Thank you for helping me find my voice. You've always been my biggest supporter even in times I couldn't see it. Providing the space to finally get this book to the finish line—both the physical space of our dream home and the space of time, has been a ginormous sacrifice. It's an honor to be your wife and partner in life. Let's go take a trip to the beach! I love you more than my words can express.

Karissa, when you arrived in this world at a whopping two pounds, our whole world changed in an instant. I was a scared twenty-four-year-old mom who didn't know much, but I sure knew I was grateful God held you in the palm of his hand to get us all through some rough beginnings. You are the apple that didn't fall far from this tree, and I'm so excited about the new season of life we get to experience together, even though we're apart. I love getting to talk to you on your drive home after work and hearing all about your new adventures. Watching you live into God's plan for your life is an incredible privilege.

Lorra, when we gave you Joy as a middle name, we had no idea just how true it would be of you! You truly spread joy everywhere you go. You are fierce, tenacious, and generous, and your optimism is incredibly contagious. Your love for travel and adventure is admirable, and I know you haven't been everywhere, though it's most definitely on your list. Your creativity and drive will serve you so well throughout life. You have so much to continue learning and so much to give. Thank you for always caring about the aesthetics when I've given up and for always finding reasons to celebrate. I love you, buddy.

Annika, you are the often quiet, dark horse of the family. I love our quality time together, whether it's a trip to the H-E-B or Target or just putting you to bed at night. I admire your discipline, patience, persistence, and ingenuity. You inspire me with your "grandma walks" and early bedtimes. Your thoughtfulness and insight never cease to amaze me. Thanks for all of the fun times we just get to hang out. I've never been a "quality time" person, but you sure make it awesome. I'm looking forward to more adventures, concerts, and desserts before dinner again soon.

Brielle, you are pure delight! Your love for music, sports, and hugs makes my heart so full! You have an incredible ability to know how others are feeling and to respond so well. You are such a good friend, and you have a heart that is so kind and tender. Keep using your voice, because it needs to be heard by the world. Thanks for being my late-night buddy as I've been writing this book and for always offering to help. I'm glad we share a love for chocolate ice cream, so let's get some to celebrate now that the book is finished, okay?

Mom, thank you for making the brave decision to get on a plane with the little you had to come to the United States from India fifty years ago. I can't even imagine how hard it was to leave your family to start brand new in a foreign land. But somewhere you knew there was so much more opportunity, and you left a comfortable life in order to pursue a great one for you and for future generations. That decision took more courage than I could ever imagine, and I'm grateful for it every day. I love you.

Carol, you are by far the most chill mother-in-law in all the land. Thank you for always being supportive of all of our crazy adventures in life. I am particularly grateful for your help in getting this book out in the eleventh hour! Thank you for sharing your love for words and writing with me!

My extended Dailey family: Colin and Lindsey, Jamin and Breezy, Stephanie, Chad and Emma—thank you for being the siblings I never had. It sure is a blast getting the entire crew together. Let's go get drinks at Copper!

Jeanne Mayo, it's time for another Cancun trip! I am so grateful to have you as a mentor, coach, consultant *and* treasured friend. Thank you for continually pointing me to Jesus and for modeling a life well lived each and every day.

Jessica Pustejovsky - you have been the most faithful of friends and an absolute gift of God in my life. You have scoured these pages more than anyone and with such joy! Without your encouragement, this book never would never have made it into the world. I know there are days I've survived only because you prayed me through them. Promise me that you'll be my friend forever, k?

Charlena Smith - your friendship is a treasure to me. Thank you for being a safe place to share my crazy ideas and helping me bring them to life. You have challenged and inspired me in ways you'll never know. I'm so excited to see all of the lives that are impacted by your family's curiosity and kindness adventures! We are long overdue for time together, so let's hop on Marco Polo and figure that out, stat!

Belinda Bauman—I love you to the summit and back again times a million googles. You will forever be my sister, and I thank God for bringing you into my life always. Wherever you go, I'm going too.

So many in the real estate industry have influenced my life and the words written in these pages: The Dailey Group, Brian and Beverly Buffini, the White Hat Community, Star Power,

Gary Keller, Keller Williams Gateway, my KW partners around the world, Joe and Leigh Bogar, Katrina Meistering, Debbie and Joe Yost, Her Best Life and the Dolls, MAPS, Wendy Papasan, CRS, the Freshies, Karina Loken, Lesley Peters, Brindley Tucker, Stephanie Evelo, Steve Schlueter, Tammi Juengst, Amanda Light, Jenn Toomer-Hay, Terrie Foster-Nowland, Debbie Frapp, John Vander Gheynst, Brian Copeland, Leigh Brown, Michael Maher, Larry Kendall, Tim Rhode, Mike Bastian, and Sam Neylan—each one of you has left an imprint on my life, and I'm grateful.

To all of my coaching clients past, present, and future—I consider it an honor to be a part of your lives for a season no matter how long or how short. I know the difference great coaches have made in my life, and I consider it the highest privilege to be invited into your world.

To all of our real estate clients we are privileged to serve, thank you for trusting us with your most precious asset—your home. To all of the Realtors who keep showing up when we teach, I promise we'll forever talk about building relationships and building community. It will *never* get old or go out of style!

To the ladies who keep showing up for girls' night out events at my home, we'll keep doing it until we run out of things to talk about! Thank you for your willingness to go deep quickly in conversation and show up authentically.

To our Austinites: Mike and Lindsay McCarthy, Justin and Jennifer Donald, Aaron and Kaleena Amuchastegui, Jon and Tatyana Vroman, Hal and Ursula Elrod, David and

Traci Osborn, Tim and Melissa Nikolaev, Les and Heatherly McDaniel, Dane and Brookelynn Espegard—thank you for making us feel so welcomed and giving us a soft place to land. Community means the world to us, and we're so grateful to have you all in our lives. Brianna Greenspan and Josh Eidenberg, you're honorary Austinites too!

I'm grateful for the communities who have impacted our lives immensely: Tony Robbins Platinum Partners, One Life, GoBundance, FamBundance, XCHANGE, the Miracle Morning Community, the Front Row Dads, Craig Groeschel and Life.Church, the Global Leadership Summit, the Empowerment Partnership, and Landmark.

Jeff and Laura Sandefer—thank you for leading the way so families like ours can thrive. You two are heroes.

Acton Academy Network—you're making a difference, one hero at a time.

Joey and Jayme Bynum—thank you for taking a chance on our crazy family!

Meredith Dew and Erika Johnson—I love you both to pieces. Suzi Dobias—thanks for keeping me healthy. You're stuck with me forever. Dr. John Ryan—you're an amazing coach. Tracy Johnson and Chris Bruno—you run the best counseling practice that exists. Thank you for teaching me how to do the "heart work." Nana Heather, thank you for welcoming our crazy family into yours! You make us all feel SO loved.

Yvette Owo—thank you for the introduction to Eric Koester! Eric, I trusted the process, and you're right, it works! Benay Stein, Rebecca Bruckenstein, Chuck Oexmann, and New Degree Press, thank you for all your efforts to make this book a reality and for believing in me all along the way.

And to you, the reader. Thank you for being on this journey. Let's make MAGIC together!

Appendix

EPIGRAPH

Doyle, Glennon. *Untamed.* New York City: The Dial Press, 2020.

AUTHOR'S NOTE

Merriam-Webster.com s.v. "entrepreneur." Accessed May 28, 2022. https://www.merriam-webster.com/dictionary/entrepreneur.

CHAPTER 1: MODEL

Mehrabian, Albert. "Silent Messages: Implicit Communication of Emotions and Attitudes." Belmont, CA: Wadsworth. 1981.

Merriam-Webster.com. s.v. "model." Accessed May 30, 2022. https://www.merriam-webster.com/dictionary/model.

CHAPTER 4: GOALS
Matthews, Gail. "The Impact of Commitment, Accountability, and Written Goals on Goal Achievement." *Psychology Faculty Presentations*.3(2007). 1-3. https://scholar.dominican.edu/psychology-faculty-conference-presentations/3.

CHAPTER 5: AFFIRM
Cascio, Christopher, Matthew Brook O'Donnell, Francis J. Tinney, Matthew D. Lieberman, Shelley E. Taylor, Victor J. Strecher, and Emily B. Falk. "Self Affirmation Activates Brain Systems Associated with Self-Related Processing and Reward and Is Reinforced by Future Orientation." *Social Cognitative and Affective Neuroscience*. (2016). 621-629. doi: 10.1093/scan/nsv136.

Online Etymology Dictionary. s.v. "affirmation." Accessed May 31, 2022. https://www.etymonline.com/word/affirmation.

Psychology Today. "Neuroplasticity." *Psychology Today*. Accessed May 1, 2022. https://www.psychologytoday.com/us/basics/neuroplasticity.

CHAPTER 8: GO
Merriam-webster.com s.v. "safety." Accessed June 1, 2022. https://www.merriam-webster.com/dictionary/safety.

CHAPTER 9: GRACE
Neff, Kristen. *Self-Compassion*. London: Hodder & Stoughton, 2013.

CHAPTER 10: TRAUMA

Angeles, Lucas. "Rewiring the Brain: How the Nervous System Heals Itself." *Vasser College. 2017.* https://www.greymattersjournalvc.org/articles/issue2/rewiringthebrain.

CHAPTER 11: BUSY

Hughes, John, dir. *Ferris Bueller's Day Off.* 1986; Los Angeles, CA: Paramount Pictures. DVD.

Online Etymology Dictionary. s.v. "decide." Accessed May 31, 2022. www.etymonline.com/word/decide.

CHAPTER 13: INQUIRE

Ainsworth-Land, George T, and Beth Jarman. 1992. *Breakpoint and beyond: Mastering the Future—Today.* Champaign, Ill.: Harperbusiness.

Carnegie, Dale. *How to Win Friends and Influence People.* New York, NY: Simon & Schuster, 1913.

Sandefer, Laura. *Courage to Grow.* Austin: Acton Press, 2020.

CHAPTER 14: EDUCATION

Sandefer, Laura. *Courage to Grow.* Austin: Acton Press, 2020.

CHAPTER 19: FAILURE
"Rocky Balboa (film) Quotes." *QuotesCosmos.com*, edited by QuotesCosmos. July 31, 2021. https://www.quotescosmos.com/quotes/Rocky-Balboa-(film)-quote-2.html.

Resources

AFFIRMATIONS

I am the architect of my life.
I am the perfect Mom for my daughter.
I am full energy and overflowing with joy.
My body is healthy, my mind is brilliant, my soul is tranquil.
I have been given endless talents which I begin to utilize today.
I forgive those who have harmed me in my past and peacefully detach from them.
I possess the qualities needed to be extremely successful.
My business and life are growing, expanding, and thriving.
Creative energy surges through me and leads me to new and brilliant ideas.
Happiness is a choice and I choose to be happy.
My ability to conquer my challenges is limitless; my potential to succeed is infinite.
I am courageous and I stand up for myself.
My thoughts are filled with positivity and my life is plentiful with prosperity.
Today, I abandon my old habits and take up new, more positive ones.
Many people look up to me and recognize my worth.
I am surrounded by an incredible family and wonderful friends.
I acknowledge my own self-worth; my confidence is soaring.
Everything that is happening now is happening for my ultimate good.
I radiate beauty, charm, and grace.
My obstacles are moving out of my way; my path is carved towards greatness.
I wake up everyday with strength in my heart and clarity in my mind.
I am at peace with all that has happened, is happening, and will happen.
My life is just beginning.
I will hold myself to a standard of grace, not perfection.
It is never too late to life a life that I love.
I find opportunity everywhere I go.

LYFEWheel

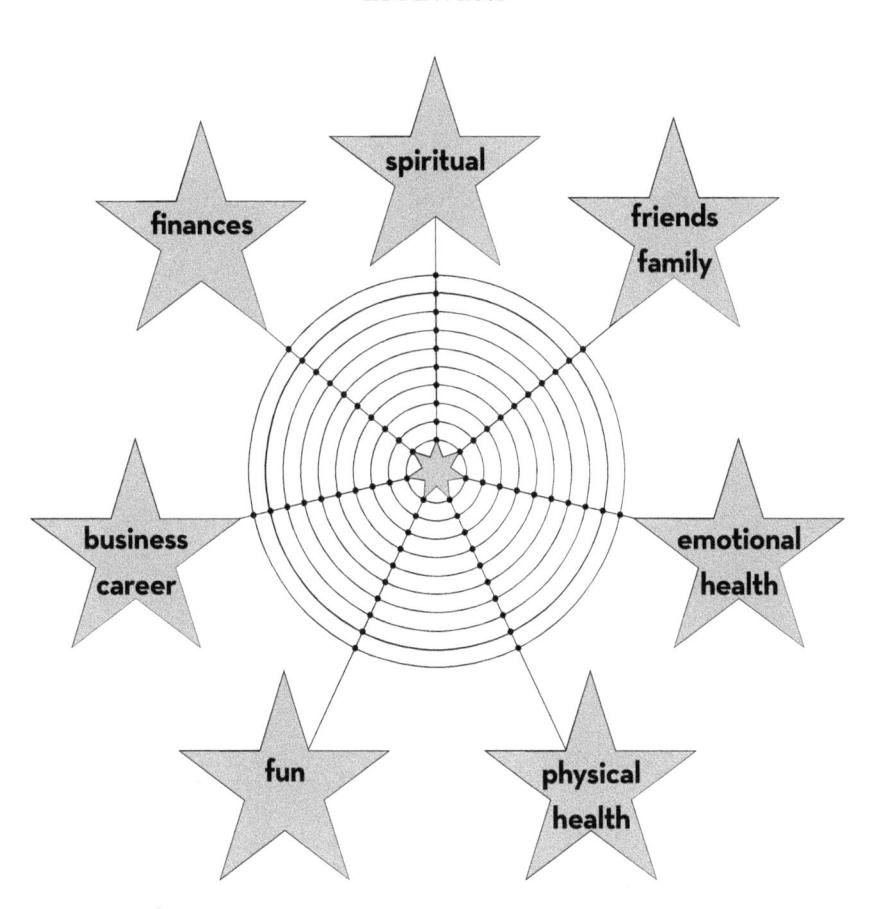

About the Author

Alyce Dailey is the ultimate Girl Mom, raising four wildly adventurous daughters while running multiple businesses alongside her husband, Seth. She has won numerous awards from *The Daily Record* and *Smart CEO* magazine for her leadership in the business community.

Having hit a wall in the midst of her flourishing career, feeling unsatisfied and with a deep desire to create a more fulfilling life, Alyce put into practice what she believed: It's never too late to design the life you want. With a flicker of hope and the rallying support of her husband and daughters, Alyce and her family picked up and moved halfway across the country to start anew.

Alyce believes that daughters don't need to see perfection in their mothers. They need to see authenticity, growth, and failure while always striving to be better. If this, too, is your heart's desire, join Alyce as she shares the wisdom she's gleaned from two decades of raising daughters to be the women who embody their calling and embrace who they were made to be.

Visit the MAGIC Momhood community and connect with other like-minded MAGIC Moms, learn more about coaching and retreats, and download free resources at www.TheMAGICMom.com.

Ready to dive deeper into becoming a MAGIC Mom?

Join other entrepreneurial Moms like you at **www.TheMAGICmomcourse.com**

CPSIA information can be obtained
at www.ICGtesting.com
Printed in the USA
LVHW080236280922
729467LV00015B/874